D1258394

REASON AND COMPASSION

REASON AND COMPASSION

The Lindsay Memorial Lectures
Delivered at the University of Keele
February-March 1971
and
The Swarthmore Lecture
Delivered to the Society of Friends
1972
by
RICHARD S. PETERS
Professor of the Philosophy of Education
The Institute of Education
University of London

ROUTLEDGE & KEGAN PAUL
London and Boston

First published in 1973
by Routledge & Kegan Paul Ltd
Broadway House, 68-74 Carter Lane,
London EC4V 5EL and
9 Park Street,
Boston, Mass. 02108, U.S.A.

Printed in Great Britain by
C. Tinling & Co. Ltd
London aud Prescot

ISBN 0 7100 7651 7 (c)
ISBN 0 7100 7652 5 (p)

Library of Congress Catalog Card No 73-80376

CONTENTS

PREFACE

THE first three of these lectures, or rather an abbreviated version of them, were first given as the Lindsay Memorial Lectures at the University of Keele in February-March 1971. Their subject-matter was chosen with due regard to Lord Lindsay's concerns; their level of presentation was determined by the mixed type of audience attending the lectures. It was hoped that they would contain some points of interest to those with a philosophical training but would also be easily intelligible to those without one.

Publication of the lectures presented problems; for they seemed too short for a monograph, but too long for an extended essay. However, the author was also asked to deliver the 1972 Swarthmore Lecture to the Society of Friends on a topic which overlapped considerably with that of the Lindsay Memorial Lectures. Much of the material of the latter was therefore used in the Swarthmore Lecture in an abridged form, with the omission of the second lecture on moral development. But in the Swarthmore Lecture there were additional sections on authority and on religion. On returning to the problem of publication presented by the Lindsay Memorial Lectures it occurred to the author that the material on religion in the Swarthmore Lecture, and its relationship to morality, if separated from its specific connection with the Quaker approach to religion, fitted in very well with the general theme of the Lindsay Memorial Lectures. It was also on a topic which was one of Lord Lindsay's abiding interests. So this material was added as a concluding chapter to make the lectures of reasonable monograph length.

The author's thanks are due to the University of Keele for the invitation to give the lectures and to the Home Service Committee of the Society of Friends for permission to reprint this material from the Swarthmore Lecture.

Lecture One

MORALITY AND MORAL DEVELOPMENT

INTRODUCTION

I feel honoured to be invited to give these lectures in memory of Lord Lindsay. I was not a Balliol man but was at Oxford at a time when Lord Lindsay exerted a powerful influence there. I remember vividly his dignified campaign as a candidate for parliament in sober contrast to the rather pink ebullience of Quintin Hogg. I also remember being considerably affected by a vigorous little book which he wrote at that time entitled *The Two Moralities*.[1]

The theme of this semi-popular work of Lord Lindsay's is very germane to the theme of these lectures. He argued soberly and sympathetically against pacifists of his day that there is a morality of 'my station and its duties' as well as an ideal morality like that put forward in the Sermon on the Mount. I, too, want to argue that morality is complex. It is not just a matter of love, or just of integrity, of 'willing one thing' as Kierkegaard put it; neither is it simply a matter of

[1] A. D. Lindsay, *The Two Moralities* (London: Eyre & Spottiswoode, 1940).

9

'my station and its duties', nor of conformity to a code; neither, finally, is it just a matter of a lonely individual making decisions that are universalizable, nor just of fixing things, as the utilitarians would have us do, with careful regard to the nicely calculated more or less. One of these aspects of morality can be emphasized against the background provided by others; but the background should not be forgotten. This is particularly important in moral education; for like Lord Lindsay I am a liberal. And as I understand it, liberalism is based on respect for the individual, which entails encouraging people to take up their own moral stance. But this policy is vacuous, educationally speaking, unless people are introduced to the moral mode of experience and come to share a complex inheritance within which they can locate and make something of themselves. What, then, is this moral mode of experience?

I CODES OR CHOICES

Unfortunately too simple a picture of it pervades the public consciousness. 'Morality', to many, still conjures up a 'code' prohibiting stealing, sex and selfishness. The very word 'code' suggests a body of rules, perhaps of an arbitrary sort, that all hang together but have no rational basis. To others, however, who are sick of triviality and stuffiness, 'morality' suggests much more individualistic and romantic notions, such as criterion-less choices, individual autonomy and subjective preferences. Whether a man experiences anguish in the attempt to be authentic, produces his 'commitment' like the white rabbit producing his watch from his waist-coat pocket, or proclaims, like Bertrand Russell in the brave old days of emotivism, that he simply does not *like* the Nazis, the picture is roughly the same—that of the romantic protest. Teachers and parents, of course, veer between these two types of extreme. If they incline towards the code conception they tend to be authoritarian in their approach; they even sometimes say, somewhat defiantly, that moral education necessarily involves a large element of indoctrination. If, on the other hand, they favour some variant of the lonely individual view of morality, they may expect that children will go it alone and decide it all for themselves. They, too, think that any attempt to instruct children in moral matters is a form of indoctrination. But, of course, they shudder at the thought of passing on anything that they may have learnt.

Surprisingly enough this over-simple presentation of the alternatives open to us is endorsed by Alasdair MacIntyre in his recent stimulating book on the history of ethics.[1] He claims that moral terms such as 'good' and 'duty' once had determinate application within a close-knit society with clear-cut purposes and well-defined roles; but now, because of social change, they have broken adrift from these concrete moorings. A pale substitute is left in generalized notions such as 'happiness' instead of determinate goals, and duty for duty's sake takes the place of role-performances that

[1] A. MacIntyre, *A Short History of Ethics* (London: Routledge & Kegan Paul, 1967).

were manifestly related to the goals of the community. So we are afflicted by a kind of moral schizophrenia in the form of irreconcilable conflicts between 'interest' and 'duty' and no clear criteria for applying these general notions, because their natural home has passed away. So, on his view, a man is either attached to one of the surviving tribalisms, or plunges around with his commitments or criterionless choices; for there is nothing else except these ancient realities to get a grip on.

Many detailed objections could be made to this highly speculative thesis for which there is no time. But in a way there is no need to chip away at its details; for there is a sense in which MacIntyre misses the point on a grand scale about the emergence of what we now call 'morality'. This is that both science and a more rational, universalistic type of morality gradually emerged precisely because social change, economic expansion and conquest led to a clash of codes and conflict between competing views of the world. At the level of life, in which discussion was encouraged to determine which story about the world was true, which code was correct, certain fundamental principles were presupposed without which the use of reason would be a mere shadow-play. I have in mind, of course, principles such as impartiality, truth-telling and freedom. In the sphere of social practices in which debates are largely about conflicting interests, there must also be assent to the principle that people's interests should be considered; for the use of reason lacks point unless it is accepted that it matters whether people suffer or satisfy their wants. And in so far as the conviction grew with the spread of Stoicism and Christianity, that a man is a citizen of the world as well as of a particular state, it came to be appreciated as well that the individual's own view about his life matters. He is not to be thought of just as an occupant of a role or as a means to the purposes of others. He should be regarded with respect, perhaps even loved, as a being with a life-space and point of view of his own.

If current codes are reflected on in the light of such principles, as happened when reflective lawyers such as Grotius tried to agree upon the laws of the sea against piracy, it comes to be seen that the content of codes are not all of a piece. There are some types of basic rules—for example, concerning contracts, non-injury, care of the young and property—which any man can see are necessary to any continuing form of social life, man being what he is and the conditions of life on earth being what they are. Above such a basic level, however, there is room for any amount of disagreement and development. Stability and consensus at a basic level are quite compatible with change and experiment at other levels. And in adjusting our stance in this way we are sensitive to fundamental principles such as fairness and the consideration of interests, which provide general criteria of relevance for moral appraisal. They prescribe the sorts of considerations that are to count as reasons. They seldom prescribe precisely what we ought to do, but at least they rule out certain courses of action and sensitize us to features of people and situations which are morally significant.

MacIntyre, it is true, applauds those like Spinoza who valued freedom and the use of reason. He admits the supreme importance of truth-telling;[1] he notes the massive consensus about basic rules for social living first emphasized by the natural law theorists, which H. L. Hart has recently revived as the bed-rock of a moral system.[2] Nevertheless, so it seems, he is unimpressed by this framework for the moral life because an appeal to such principles and basic rules cannot give specific guidance to any individual who is perplexed about what he ought to do. But why this emphasis on the predicament of the perplexed? Why should this feature of moral life be accorded so much importance at the expense of the emergence of general criteria for assessing people and situations? Why this hankering for unambiguous directions? Of course, any adequate moral theory must account for the palpable fact that morally sensitive people disagree over a range of issues. But it must also account for the measure of agreement —not only about substantive issues, but also about the sorts of considerations that are admitted to be relevant in making up our minds. If we are discussing the merits of gambling we do not dwell approvingly or disapprovingly on the amount of greenness in the world brought about by the construction of card-tables. If we

[1] See A. MacIntyre, op. cit., pp. 95–6.

[2] See H. L. Hart, *The Concept of Law* (Oxford University Press, 1961), chs. VIII and IX.

think a man wicked it is not normally in virtue of his height.

The fundamental feature of this form of life, which MacIntyre completely ignores, is that an attempt is made to base conduct and assessment of people on reasons which fall under principles which make them relevant. In the history of man this is a rare phenomenon. The more usual practice has been to rely on tradition or on some authoritative source, as in most religions. This way of conducting life developed precisely because there was a clash between codes which had a traditional or authoritative basis. When faced with discrepant demands, men had to reflect, to go behind 'convention' to 'nature' or some other standard which would provide a universal basis for adjudicating between such codes. And in coming together in this way men *presupposed* certain principles such as impartiality, freedom, truth-telling, the consideration of interests and respect for persons which provided general criteria by reference to which they could weigh up different codes of conduct. A *form* of experience gradually emerged under which contents deriving from different traditions were fitted. This form of experience is what I call 'rational morality'.

2 ETHICAL EMPHASES

Rational morality, like science, took a long time to emerge, to become distinguished from religion, law and custom. It was not until the seventeenth and eighteenth centuries that its main features were made explicit. Moral philosophers such as Locke, Butler, Hume, Kant, Price and Mill contributed much to this process. But, as they were concerned with justification as well as with tracing the contours of a form of life, they underpinned it with different epistemological theories, which required that some features had to be emphasized because they were thought of as justificatory grounds for others. What, then, are these main features?

There is, first of all, as MacIntyre points out, the typically Greek element. Man has certain wants and takes part in characteristic activities, for which he usually demands freedom. It is in this sphere that terms such as 'good', 'desirable', 'worthwhile' have obvious application, and omnibus terms such as 'well-being' and 'interests' are used to characterize this area as a whole.

Second, under concepts such as 'obligation' and 'duty' fall ways of behaving connected with social roles. Much of a person's life is taken up with his station and its duties, with what is socially required of him as a husband, father, citizen, and member of a profession or occupation. This, perhaps, is the more Roman element.

Third, there are rules, more prominent in an open society, which are not specifically connected with any social role but which govern conduct between people generally. Duties such as those of fairness, unselfishness and honesty are examples. These affect the manner in which a person conducts himself within his activities and roles as well as in his non-institutionalized dealings with others. They are personalized as character-traits.

Fourth, there are equally wide-ranging goals of life which are personalized in the form of 'motives'. These point to purposes not confined to particular activities or roles which derive from non-neutral appraisals of a situation. Examples are ambition, benevolence, envy, greed, love and respect.

Finally, there are very general traits of character which embody not so much the rules a man follows or the purposes which he pursues as the manner in which he follows or pursues them. On the one hand, there are those connected with 'the will' in which courses of action are followed in the face of counter-inclinations. Examples are determination, integrity, conscientiousness and consistency. On the other hand are human excellences, such as autonomy, creativeness, wisdom, and so on, which depend on the development of rational capacities.

Moral philosophers have tried to impose some sort of unity on this rather complex heritage, usually by fastening on one or two features of it and trying to justify the rest in terms of the principles which seemed applicable to them. The Utilitarian, for instance, takes the first sphere of the good as his starting point and picks out as a principle some general account of its pursuit—for example, the pursuit of happiness or interests, or worthwhile activities. Duties connected with role-performances and the following of more general social rules are then justified by references to their tendency to promote the interests of all. But notorious problems break out in Utilitarianism about the status of special obligations and the general duties of fairness and truth-telling. The moral significance of the individual's inner state, too, becomes problematic. Witness Mill's problems about motives. And virtues such as integrity and conscientiousness either go by the board or an implausible Utilitarian case is run up for them. The truth of the matter is that Utilitarianism was basically the legislator's emphasis in morality. It has an important contribution to make in the public realm of social roles and practices but seems out of place in more personal spheres. It emphasizes just one principle that makes reasons relevant—that of the consideration of interests.

The Kantian view has a better coverage. As it was a system erected on the lonely will of the individual confronted with choice, integrity, conscientiousness and autonomy are prominent. The principle of impartiality provides the criterion by reference to which his 'subjective maxims' coming from different codes can be justified. And a case can be made for certain types of duties like promise-keeping when this test is applied. But the realm of 'the good' is rather down-graded and much of social morality, including role-performances, is left in a dubious state, when only this abstract test is applied. As morality is conceived of as a matter of the rational will, there is a problem, too, about the status of motives such as benevolence and love, if it is of the 'pathological' type. On this view moral worth is an *achievement.* A man who has a genuine concern for others is nice to have around; but he has no moral merit if it comes naturally to him. One motive, however, namely respect, is given a special status in order to plug this gap in the system.

Then there are intuitionists, such as Butler, Price and Ross, who despair of seeing any unity in the moral life but claim that various principles are self-evident to any rational man. Regard to the common good or the consideration of interests is usually amongst them; so are fairness and truth-telling. Ross also adds gratitude from the realm of motives and promise-keeping from that of special obligations. His list of prima facie obligations is indeed a motley selection; but it bears witness to the pressure on him of the different realms of the moral life, and of the different principles definitive of a rational way of proceeding.

There are also ethical positions which I can regard only as partial pleas for particular spheres of life or features of rationality that are tending to be overlooked. Amongst these I would put Bradley's plea for 'my station and its duties' and Kierkegaard's plea for integrity or purity of heart.

In many ways the most satisfactory system of all, because of its comprehensiveness, was that of David Hume. Significantly he was not ostensibly concerned with justification—only with making explicit what he found to be implicit in the moral judgments of his contemporaries. Impartiality was prominent in his system; for he claimed that moral judgments are made from the point of view of 'the impartial spectator'. But they are directed towards mental qualities or dispositions which are agreeable or useful to their possessor or to society, or the reverse. But these judgments are not all of a piece. On the one hand, we have *admiration* or the reverse for the individual in his pursuit of what is good. This covers both the first realm that I distinguished of worthwhile activities and those qualities of character such as integrity, enterprise, courage, and the like which are shown in the manner of his conduct. On the other hand, there are qualities which are useful to society, of which we *approve*, such as justice and benevolence. Within this group Hume made an important distinction between natural virtues, springing from universal motives such as benevolence, which are immediately and universally approved by the impartial spectator, and conventional virtues, such as justice, which are approved of because their social utility is recognized. This is an important point; for Hume ascribed virtue to people with certain sorts of motives, irrespective of whether effort is required for them to be operative. Not all goodness requires the exercise of will. The details of Hume's systematization can, of course, be questioned—for instance, his implausible account of the status of justice. Fundamental objections, too, can be raised to his thin account of reason and to his contention that the reaction of the impartial spectator, which Kant transformed into the universalization test of practical reason, is appropriately described as a disinterested passion. But the point is that Hume's system does take account of all the spheres of morality that I have mentioned, and does attempt to unify them by introducing, albeit as disinterested passions, principles which are fundamental to the use of reason.

In modern ethical systems there are similar differences in emphasis. There are Kantian philosophers of the lonely will, such as Hare, who attempt to erect an ethical edifice on the narrow plank of the individual sincerely assenting to principles that have passed the universalization test; then there is the more Utilitarian approach of Toulmin who, taking the model of science, thinks of the moral life as mainly a matter of applying tests to social practices. Religion has to be introduced to put some heart into the moral life. Then, finally, there is Iris Murdoch's recent critique of Kantian and Utilitarian systems. Her system starts off in Humean fashion by making the appreciation of virtue central, the just and loving assessment by the spectator of the individual. She then rather takes off into Platonic realms. Much that is usually ascribed to the use of reason is swept up into the love of the good. But there is practically no mention of the more public and political area of the moral life.

Whether or not these various elements in the moral life can be completely unified is a further question to which I will return at the end of this lecture. Perhaps MacIntyre is right in suggesting that we are bound, to a certain extent, to be pulled apart by their discrepant demands. At this juncture I only wish to make two main points. The first is that a rational morality emerged in part as a response to conflict between traditionally held codes or religions. A measure of moral disagreement is not, therefore, an *objection* to postulating its existence. Thinkers like Grotius, for instance, were sick of the conflict and wars stemming from competing religions. Their search for a basic set of rules marked an attempt to get away from a traditionally held or authoritatively based code and presupposed some agreement on what I have called fundamental principles—for example, freedom, fairness, truth-telling and the consideration of interests, without which the attempt to reason about personal conduct or social practices would never get properly off the ground. So, although the various attempts to systematize morality grant a different status to these principles, some place is usually found for them; for they are presuppositions of being reasonable.

Second, the moral life must have content as well as procedural principles for reasoning about what one is to do, be, or think. *Some* account, therefore, has to be given of what a man's interests are, of the realm of the pursuit of what is good or worthwhile. Since, too much of a man's life is spent as an occupant of a role, in taking part in institutionalized social practices, something must be said about a man's station and its duties. And, finally, in any society in which individuals are thought to matter, in which there is any extension of duties beyond role performances and in which relationships between man and man are emphasized, some account must be given of character traits such as un-selfishness and meanness and of motives such as pride, jealousy and benevolence. Something, too, must be said about virtues such as integrity and courage which embody the manner in which an admired individual goes about his life.

3 MORAL DEVELOPMENT

So far I have been concerned only with the emergence of rational morality as a form of experience made explicit by the work of moral philosophers. I have pointed to its contrast with traditional or authoritatively based forms of conduct and have stressed that its form is connected with the appeal to certain principles that it presupposes. I have also tried to show how it permits different emphases which are closely connected with the diverse contents for which it provides an organizing form.

A parallel to this historical evolution can be found in facts of child development as revealed by Piaget and later by Kohlberg who confirmed Piaget's findings by cross-cultural studies. There is variability in the content of morality but an invariant sequence in the development of its *form*, which, in the life of the individual, parallels the transition from traditional and authoritatively based moralities to rational morality. But here again it can be argued that different *emphases* are possible within the form that finally emerges. In briefly expounding these findings I will concentrate on Kohlberg's refinement of Piaget's theory.

Kohlberg[1] claims, on the basis of his investigations in many countries, that although there is a difference between cultures in the *content* of moral beliefs, their *form* is a cultural invariant. There are, in other words, cultural variations with regard to thrift, punctuality, sexual relationships, and so on, but there are cross-cultural uniformities in how such rules are conceived. Children start by seeing rules as dependent upon power and external compulsion; they then see them as instrumental to rewards and to the satisfaction of their needs; then as ways of obtaining social approval and esteem; then as upholding some ideal order, and finally as articulations of social principles necessary to living together with others—especially that of justice. Varying contents given to rules are fitted into invariant forms of conceiving of rules.

Of course, in many cultures there is no progression through to the final stage of autonomy; the rate of development differs and in the same culture there are great individual differences. All this can be granted and explained. But his main thesis is unaffected. This sequence in levels of conceiving of rules is constitutive of moral development and it is a cultural invariant. Its form is universal because, so Kohlberg argues, development is not the product of teaching. The ways of conceiving, characterizing the different levels of development, form a logical hierarchy. Moral understanding

[1] L. Kohlberg, 'Stage and sequence: the cognitive-developmental approach to socialization', in D. Goslin (ed.), *Handbook of Socialization* (Chicago, Rand McNally, 1968).

proceeds from the heteronomous stage, when rules are regarded as, 'out there', laid down by the peer-group or parents, to the autonomous stage when questions of their validity can be entertained and their basis in reciprocity and consent discerned, just as in the scientific sphere, the Aristotelian stage of classification makes way for the Galilean stage of hypothetico-deductive thinking. In both spheres, he argues, development could not be in any other order, although it can be retarded or accelerated by social factors. Hence the cultural invariance.

I will leave aside until my next lecture Kohlberg's interactionist theory of development. I wish to concentrate purely on the features of the ethical emphasis which is implicit in this theory of development. There is little need to point out that it is a Kantian one, for Piaget's whole approach is Kantian. Thus the significant feature of moral development is found to be the individual's way of conceiving of rules; the supreme virtue is that of justice which regulates, in an abstract way, the autonomous person's assessment of rules. It is claimed, too, that ego-strength, evidence for which is found in the tendency to anticipate future events, the ability to maintain focused attention, the capacity to control unsocialized fantasies and self-esteem, is also correlated with moral development. What emerges as the end-point of moral development is the autonomous individual acting on principles that can be universalized and with the strength of will to stick to them.

This suffers, as an account of development, from the

defects of the Kantian approach. There is an exclusive
interest in how the individual conceives of interpersonal
rules. This is what the Piagetian type of test elicits from
the subjects of investigation. There is no probing of the
motives that explain their actions, no assessment of the
intensity or level of compassion which suffuses their
dealings with others. Yet this, surely, is developmentally most important; for what is the moral status
of a man who can reason in an abstract way about rules
if he does not *care* about people who are affected by
his breach or observance of them? How do people
come to care in this way? In the Piaget-Kohlberg
theory there is not even much attention to the development of the Kantian emotion of respect. So if their
subjects showed little ability to think abstractly about
rules and actions but were very warm-hearted and
compassionate in their attitude to others, where would
they be, developmentally speaking? Is not the capacity
to love, as well as the capacity to reason, important in
the form of morality? Does it not transform a person's
role-performances and dealing with others? Must not
some developmental account be given of Hume's
'sentiment for humanity'?

4 THE UNITY OF THE MORAL LIFE

The fact that the Piaget-Kohlberg theory of moral
development concentrates only on the form of the
moral life viewed rather narrowly in terms of the way
in which rules are conceived and in the manner in
which they are followed, that is, on ego-strength or

strength of will, does not mean that this feature of development cannot be combined with others in a less one-sided account of moral development. Indeed, as was remarked before, a more Humean account can be given of the moral life in which the virtue of justice can occupy a prominent place, but in which more room is made for what Hume called 'the natural virtues' stemming from the sentiment of humanity. The question is whether the development of reason and of concern for others are sufficient to provide some kind of unity to the moral life so conceived.

A combination of the two could possibly be deployed, as by Hume, to impose a loose type of unity on the different areas of the moral life which provide its content. There is, first of all, a long tradition of thought going back to Plato which stresses the importance of reason in the pursuit of good—in the delay of gratification, in the planning of means to ends, and the avoidance of conflict by the imposition of coherence and consistency on the pursuit of ends. A much more controversial case can be made for saying that pursuits which are to be regarded as admirable and good in themselves, are ones in which various rational capacities and attitudes are exercised—that is, those requiring skill, judgment, care and a concern for standards.[1]

[1] See R. S. Peters, 'The justification of education', in R. S. Peters (ed.), *The Philosophy of Education* (Oxford University Press, 1973); and J. Passmore, *The Perfectibility of Man* (London: Duckworth, 1970), chs 14 and 15.

The area of roles, interpersonal rules and social practices presents much diversity of content. But this can be unified by rejecting what is indefensible when looked at in the light of considerations deriving from principles, such as impartiality, freedom, truth-telling and the consideration of interests which are presuppositions of the exercise of practical reason, if these principles are applied with concern for individuals.

In the area of virtues and vices the same sorts of considerations will surely be relevant. Some of them such as punctuality and tidiness, embody rules of interpersonal conduct and can be assessed in the same sort of way as social practices, such as gambling. Others, such as jealousy, avarice and pity, are motives or emotions. Those which are disapproved of as vices are mainly those which involve harm or unfairness to others or lack of respect or concern for them. Motives which we regard as virtues are surely those which exemplify that disinterestedness and concern for what is 'out there' which is a feature shared by both reason and concern for others. What Koestler calls 'self-transcending emotions'[1]—for example, awe, wonder, pity, respect and reverence—are pre-eminent examples of emotions which share the same fundamental feature.

Finally, the virtues connected with 'the will'—for example, courage, integrity and perseverance—are connected with rationality, with consistency, and with the maxim that to will the end is to will the means. But

[1] A. Koestler, *The Act of Creation* (London: Pan Books, 1964), p. 55.

what is distinctive of them is that various forms of rationality are exercised in the face of counter-inclinations. And excellences such as autonomy, creativeness and wisdom are manifestly developments of rational capacities.

But although reason and concern for others can thus work together to provide a loose kind of unity for a form of life, there is surely the possibility that they may be, in certain respects, incompatible in their respective demands and may pull the individual in different directions. This possibility must now briefly be considered. They work together over a wide area of life because a certain similarity is to be discerned between them. This emerges imaginatively from Miss Murdoch's stimulating, but rather undiscriminating, account of love of the good.[1] They share a certain disinterestedness and concern for what is 'out there'. In the case of reason, because its point is to discover what is true, there must be humility in the face of facts and evidence, a respect for how things are. Because of the determination to follow the argument, impartiality is essential; for what is true depends on the considerations which are adduced, not on the personal position or characteristics of anyone who adduces them. But this disinterestedness is *generalised*; for in the use of reason, particularities of time, place and identity are irrelevant. In concern for others, on the other hand, the concentration is away from the self, but it may be directed towards the

[1] See I. Murdoch, *The Sovereignty of Good* (London: Routledge & Kegan Paul, 1970).

particular features of the person who is its object. Miss Murdoch rightly compares 'love' in this sense to the attitude appropriate to contemplating a work of art. The object is seen as it is unclouded by the observer's narcissistic preoccupations; but it is dwelt on in its particularity.

There are thus two obvious ways in which an individual may be pulled in a divergent direction by the Christian as distinct from the Stoic legacy within this form of life. First, there may be conflicts, as Hume saw only too clearly, between what he called limited benevolence and justice. Second, the individual may make concern for others and the development of personal relationships with them his main preoccupation in life. It may become for him what science is to the dedicated scientist—a supremely worthwhile activity. And this may lead at times to that unreasonableness which is exhibited in forgoing claims and being oblivious to normal considerations of prudence. For prudence is a virtue of bishops and administrators rather than of saints.

It could be argued, however, that the Christian and Stoic ideals of life cannot be adequately represented without some concession to the dominant emphasis of the other. The Stoic, for instance, has *some* kind of concern for the individual which affects the way in which he applies his principles. But this takes the form of respect. In this attitude another individual is viewed as a possessor of rational capacities, as a centre of evaluation and choice. The thought of him as an individual, who has a point of view and who is, to a certain extent, a determiner of his own destiny, is affectively tinged. But he is viewed under these very *general* descriptions without necessarily any sense of his uniqueness. Neither need there be any *warming* to him as an individual, any outgoingness towards him. Indeed, respect for persons is compatible with a purely negative determination not to exploit someone or to treat him purely as an occupant of a role. Nevertheless, though involving these general aspects, respect is an attitude directed towards *individuals* which is essential to the stress on reason in the Stoic emphasis. In the Christian emphasis, on the other hand, though love may be highly particularized, it is not altogether immune in its operation from rational considerations. People may be loved as individuals in their uniqueness; they may not be loved under any general descriptions, but such love is criticizable if it is based on false beliefs. If, too, it leads to conduct that is grossly unfair to someone else, that is a fault. In other words, concessions have to be made to the claims of reason. These can be summarized in the saying that love may transcend but does not supplant the law.

It can be argued, therefore, that just as the Stoic must make some room in his system for compassion, so the Christian must make some room for the influence of reason. Nevertheless, there can be great differences in emphasis. The Stoic sees life mainly in terms of rules, disciplining his emotions by reflection, and the development of those attitudes that support a reflective way of life. The Christian, on the other hand, sees life much more in terms of states of mind which can be transformed by love. He admits the necessity of rules but sees them mainly as providing a framework for the moral life rather than as its substance. Thus, after a long journey, we return to my starting point—Lord Lindsay's essay in which he pointed to the possible irreconcilability of distinct emphases within the moral life. I have not represented the tension as being between the demands of love and those of 'my station and its duties'. For this mundane conception of morals surely provides only a stable *content* to morality which can rest either on tradition or on rational considerations based on principles. Love or concern for others, on the other hand, has been represented, like reason, as being an important aspect of the *form* of morality which can underpin and transform content connected with roles, rules and the emotional life. The real tension is between the generalized demands of reason and the particularized promptings of compassion. These are both elements in the form of the moral mode of experience which we have inherited. The distinction, however, between the content of the moral life and the form of the moral consciousness is a very important one in the context of moral development and moral learning. This will be the subject of my next lecture.

Lecture Two

MORAL DEVELOPMENT
AND MORAL LEARNING

THERE are many puzzles about learning in general and moral learning in particular, but two seem of particular importance to the educator. The first is called the paradox of moral education which is as old as Aristotle. It is really the paradox of all education. Common sense tells us that the things which we have to learn to do we learn to do by doing them. Just as men become builders by building, so men become honest by being honest. Habit-formation, in other words, plays an important part in moral learning. Yet there is a very great difference between the way in which the morally mature person conceives of honesty and the way in which the learner conceives of the acts by means of which he becomes honest. How can a rational level of morality emerge from this lowly level of habit-formation?

The second puzzle is the violent divergence between psychologists and educators about human learning which seldom leads to a decisive confrontation. Instruction-based teachers and Skinnerians are insistent on the success of their methods. The advocates of experience and discovery are equally enthusiastic about *their* methods and claim the authority of Piaget to support them. The debate reverberates through classrooms and common-rooms, and both sides can draw on experience and experiments to support their case. Could it not be that they are both right but that they are really interested in different aspects of learning? If this were so it might be possible to point the way both to a reconciliation between these different approaches to learning and to avoiding the paradox of education.

The key to such a reconciliation is to be found in the Kantian type of distinction that I have made between the form of moral experience and its content. This distinction is made explicitly by Kohlberg, following Piaget, but as he is interested only in the development of the form of experience rather than in the learning of content there is a one-sided emphasis in his theory. Kohlberg admits that the *content* of rules—for example, about honesty, punctuality and tidiness—is learnt by instruction and imitation, aided by rewards and punishment, praise and blame. But he is not interested in such habit-formation; for he claims that such habits are short-term and situation-specific. They are of minor importance in moral development which depends on how rules are conceived rather than on cultural content. There is a transition from conceiving of rules as connected with rewards and punishments to conceiving of them as 'out there' backed by praise and blame from the peer-group and authority figures, and finally to conceiving of them as alterable conventions depending upon consent and reciprocity. Development depends not upon explicit teaching, backed by reinforcement, but upon the interaction of the child with his social environment, which is aided or retarded by the amount of 'cognitive stimulation' available to the child which helps him to conceive of the social environment in the required manner.

Kohlberg's claims about how the form of moral experience develops and about the role of 'cognitive stimulation' are of obvious importance in the context of my interest in the emergence of a rational form of morality. So are their implications for the learning of content; for the level of conception determines both the type of content that can be assimilated and the aids which are available for this assimilation. In other words the type of 'reinforcement' used by Skinnerians can be shown to be peculiarly appropriate to learning specific types of *content* at certain stages of development. If it is important that the child should assimilate a certain type of content—for example, rules about not stealing—there may only be certain ways in which this can be done at a certain age—for example, by being rewarded or praised for conformity. So Skinnerians may be right about the learning of content. But learning the *form* of experience may be a very different matter. And some methods of teaching content might impede the child from developing to a stage at which a different conception of rules is possible.

This distinction between the development of the form of morality and the learning of its content is, therefore, crucial in what I have to say about moral learning. So I will now try to sketch some of the details of moral learning first of all in relation to the form of morality and then in relation to its content.

2 THE FORM OF MORALITY

(a) *Becoming a chooser*

The first stage of development in morality is concerned with the acquisition of a basic cognitive and affective apparatus without which a man could not qualify as a moral agent in the full sense, a chooser rather than a being beset by various forms of irrationality. He must be able to delay gratification, to decide what to do in the light of publicly assessable reasons instead of only following lines dictated by some irrational wish or aversion, and to act after deliberation without being paralysed by indecision. These capacities presuppose the development of the type of categoreal apparatus with which Piaget, following Kant, was concerned. The individual has to be able to think in terms of taking means to an end. He must appreciate, to a certain extent, the causal properties of things and must distinguish consequences brought about by his own agency from those that come about independently of his will. To do this he must possess the categoreal concepts of 'thinghood', 'causality' and 'means to an end'. These enable him to think 'realistically' in contradistinction to small children and paranoiacs whose consciousness is dominated by wishes and aversions. It presupposes, too, that he has a view of the world as an orderly system in which his confidence in his own powers and his expectations about the future will be confirmed.

(i) *Specific teaching and cognitive stimulation* Now followers of Piaget have been most energetic in demonstrating that this framework of concepts, necessary for rational thought and choice, cannot be imparted by specific teaching. The child has to be provided with plenty of concrete experience. He will gradually come to grasp these organizing notions if he is suitably stimulated like the slave in *The Meno*. And there is a sense in which both these contentions must be true; for what is being learnt is a *principle*, which provides unity to a number of previously disconnected experiences. This has to be 'seen' or grasped by the individual and it cannot be grasped as a principle unless the individual is provided with experience of the items which it unifies. If information is being imparted which has to be memorized, the teacher can instruct the learner explicitly in what has to be learnt; in learning a skill the particular movements can be demonstrated explicitly for the learner to copy or practice. But if the teacher is trying to get the learner to grasp a principle, all he can do is to draw attention to common features of cases and hope that the penny will drop. Also, once the child has grasped the principle, he knows how to go on, as Wittgenstein put it; there is thus no limit to the number of cases that he will see as falling under the principle. There is a sense, therefore, in which the learner gets out much more than any teacher could have put in. Kohlberg's objection to *specific* teaching is therefore readily explained; for principles just are not the sorts of things that can be applied only to a specific number of items which could be imparted by a teacher.

Kohlberg, of course, is using 'teaching' in a very specific sense to mean something like 'explicit instruction'. It is only this very narrow conception of 'teaching' which can be properly contrasted with 'cognitive stimulation'; for most people would say that Socrates was teaching the slave in *The Meno* even though he was not explicitly telling him things. And manifestly everything that Kohlberg says about appropriate 'cognitive stimulation' bears witness to the importance of social influences in the acquisition of this cognitive structure, however broadly or narrowly 'teaching' is to be conceived. For, leaving aside problematic Chomsky-type questions about the extent to which this cognitive structure is innately determined, the influence of social factors which are connected with such 'stimulation' can be inferred from the fact that the failure to develop such a structure has been shown by psychologists of the Freudian school to be connected with certain types of socialization, or the lack of it.

(ii) *The influence of social conditions*   Most pathological states can be described in terms of the absence of features of this structure and these defects can be correlated with typical conditions in early childhood. It is generally agreed, for instance, that psychopaths who live on their whims and impulses, for whom the future has little reality, are largely the product of homes which are rejecting towards the child and which provide a very inconsistent type of discipline.[1] Schizophrenics, whose belief-structure in regard to their own identity is deranged, are thought by some to be products of discrepant and irreconcilable attitudes towards them before they developed a secure sense of reality. They lack what Laing calls the 'ontological security' of a person who has developed the categoreal apparatus which is definitive of being a rational being or a chooser,[2] 'a sense of his integral selfhood and personal identity, of the permanency of things, of the reliability of natural processes, of the substantiality of others.'

There is no need to multiply examples of failures to develop the apparatus necessary for becoming a chooser and to attempt to relate them to various types of defects in 'normal social conditions'. To do this thoroughly would necessitate writing a textbook on psychopathology. Of equal interest, however, from the point of view of educators, are cases of people who may be termed 'unreasonable' rather than 'irrational' and whose way of life bears witness to the limited development of the capacities necessary for being a chooser, which again seem to be the product of a certain type of socialization. An example of such a limited form of

[1] See, for instance, R. F. Peck and R. J. Havighurst, *The Psychology of Character Development* (New York: Wiley, 1960), pp. 109–11.

[2] R. D. Laing, *The Divided Self* (Harmondsworth: Penguin Books, 1965), p. 39.

development is given by Josephine Klein.[1] She singles out certain abilities which are important in the development of reasoning—the ability to abstract and use generalizations, the ability to perceive the world as an ordered universe in which rational action is rewarded, the ability to plan ahead and to exercise self-control. She cites evidence from Luria and Bernstein to show that the extent to which these abilities develop depends on the prevalence of an elaborated form of language which is found in some strata of society but not in others. She also shows how the beliefs and conduct of some working-class subcultures are affected by the arbitrariness of their child-rearing techniques. Such happy-go-lucky people have a stunted capacity for choice because the future has only a limited significance for them, and because their lack of generalizations limits their view of possibilities. They are prejudiced, myopic and unreflective in their beliefs.

It need hardly be added that these rational capacities can be neutralized, perhaps permanently impaired, by more conscious techniques which are combined together in brain-washing. The individual's categoreal apparatus can be attacked by making his environment as unpredictable as possible; his sense of time and place and of his own identity can be systematically undermined. He is gradually reduced to a state of acute anxiety, perhaps of mental breakdown, in which he is in a receptive state to being dominated by another who

[1] J. Klein, *Samples of English Culture* (London: Routledge & Kegan Paul, 1965), 2 vols.

becomes the sole source of pleasure and security for him. He becomes suggestible and willing to accept beliefs which, in his former life, he would have rejected out of hand. He becomes more or less a programmed man rather than a chooser.

It is not difficult to surmise why the most consistent finding from studies of child-rearing practices is that sensible children, who are capable of rational choice, seem to emerge from homes in which there is a warm attitude of acceptance towards children, together with a firm and consistent insistence on rules of behaviour without much in the way of punishment. An accepting attitude towards a child will tend to encourage trust in others and confidence in the child's own powers. A predictable social environment will provide the type of experience which is necessary for guiding behaviour by reflection on its consequences and so build up a belief in a future which is, in part, shaped by the child's own behaviour. Inconsistency in treatment, on the other hand, will encourage plumping for rather than choosing and attachment to instant gratification; and a rejecting attitude will inhibit the development of the self-confidence which is necessary for being a chooser.

(iii) *The development of 'the sentiment for humanity'*
If, however, we consider cases of moral failure such as those of psychopaths or of people with very little strength of will, we are impressed not simply by their lack of the normal apparatus for reasoning; they also seem lacking in strength of feeling for others which would enable them to control their hankering for

instant gratification. The findings of the Piagetian school, which confirm Aristotle's paradox, is that at a very early age children cannot grasp reasons for types of action in the sense that they cannot connect a practice such as that of stealing with considerations such as the harm to others brought about by such a practice. In other words, concern for others cannot serve as a *principle* for them. But this does not show that very early on they cannot genuinely feel concern for others. If they are sensitive to the suffering of others early on the hope is that, with the development of their capacity for reasoning, this will later be one of the main features of the form of their moral life, as I argued in my first lecture.

How, then, do children come to feel concern for others? Is there an innate basis for it in sympathy? Is Money-Kyrle[1] right in arguing that the origins of what he calls the 'humanistic conscience' (Hume's 'sentiment for humanity') which Freud neglected, are to be found in the child's early relationships with his mother? Does not this type of guilt need to be distinguished from the guilt which is the product of punishment and of internalized social disapproval? And does not its development need to be carefully studied? There is no answer to this type of question in the Piaget-Kohlberg theory. Yet a developmental account of concern for others is surely as important as a developmental account of reasoning and of the child's

[1] R. Money-Kyrle, *Psycho-analysis and Politics* (London: Duckworth, 1931).

attitude to rules. In this area of moral development the findings of Piaget surely need to be supplemented by those of the Freudian and social learning schools of psychology. For there is considerable evidence to suggest that the child's capacity for sympathy and his trust in others depends very much on the pattern of his early social relationships. The Piagetian type of approach has much to say about how concern for others can become more realistic, and about the general influence of reversibility in thought on such feelings— that is, when a child can see something from someone else's point of view. But it leaves obscure questions about the origin and intensity of such feelings.

(b) Code-encased morality

At the first level of development the child, as I have explained, is acquiring the general apparatus for reasoning and the beginnings of concern for others. But his attitude to rules is basically egocentric; he sees conformity with them basically as a way of avoiding punishment and of obtaining rewards.[1] At the next 'transcendental' stage of moral realism a rule comes to be seen as a rule and to depend for its existence on the will of the peer-group and of authority figures. This is a crucial stage in moral development; for it involves the realization on the part of the child of what it is to follow a rule, to accept a rule as a rule binding on one's

---

[1] Kohlberg divides this egocentric stage into two, avoidance of punishment coming before the seeking of rewards. Similarly, the second stage of moral realism is divided into two—that of peer-group conformity and authority-based morality.

conduct. Much of what Freud wrote about the super-
ego relates surely to this stage, although he was concerned more with exaggerated and distorted types of
'internalization' rather than with the normal developmental process of coming to accept a rule as a rule.[1] At
this stage of development children come to enjoy
following rules and to revel in the sense of mastery
that this gives them. They have as yet no notion of the
validity of rules. They regard them as just there,
supported by the approval of the peer-group and of
authority figures. This rather second-hand, take-it-on-
trust attitude pervades their participation in activities
which are later to be constituents in their conception of
personal good, as well as in their emotional life. It is a
period at which imitation and identification are extremely important in learning. And the forms of
motivation available to them parallel their conception
of activities and rules. They either learn things if they
can view them somewhat as games that have rules to be
mastered or in so far as they see the connection between
correct performance and social approval and disapproval.

This stage of rule-conformity is a very important
one in moral development. In the USSR Makarenko
achieved considerable success in dealing with delinquents by reliance mainly on group projects and on
identification with the collective will of the com-

[1] See R. S. Peters, 'Freud's theory of moral development in
relation to that of Piaget', *Brit. Journ. Ed. Psych.*, xxx, Part iii,
November 1960.

munity.[1] As presumably most of these delinquents were either at the first egocentric stage or suffering from various pathological conditions, it was a distinct sign of moral advancement for these individuals to function at the second stage of morality at which the individual does the done thing, which is determined either by the group or by those in authority. If Piaget and Kohlberg are right, however, in their assumptions about the development of autonomy, *every* individual has to go through this stage of what Kohlberg calls 'good boy' morality before he can attain the autonomous stage. The public schools, who specialized in character-training, implicitly acknowledged this; for they combined an appeal to team spirit and not letting the house down for all, with an emphasis on independence of mind and sticking to principles for those more senior boys who were singled out to command rather than simply to obey. It is questionable whether progressive educators have been sufficiently aware of the importance of this second stage of development. They have, on the one hand, been reluctant for the staff to impose the rule of law but have been embarrassed by the fact that, if this is withdrawn, bullying and peer-group pressures take its place. On the other hand, they have emphasized the importance of individual choice without paying enough attention to the developmental stage which individual children have reached. Unless a child has been through the second stage of

[1] See F. Lilge, *Anton Semyonovitch Makarenko* (University of California Press, 1958), especially pp.25–6.

morality, at which he understands from the inside what a rule is and has some feeling about the inviolability of rules, it is dubious whether the notion of adopting his own rules is very meaningful to him.

In the history of man, development beyond this stage of morality to a third or autonomous stage is probably a rare phenomenon, depending on the development of what Popper has called an 'open society'. Within our own type of society Kohlberg himself stresses the differences in rate of development beyond the second stage of those who come from middle-class, as distinct from working-class, homes. There is, too, a series of investigations by Bruner and his associates which are far-reaching in their implications for the importance of social influences; for they show not only how individuals pass to the second stage, but also how they are massively discouraged from passing beyond it.

Bruner conducted experiments into ideas about conservation with the Wolof, a tribe in Senegal, and found that those who have not been exposed to western influences embodied in schooling, tend to adopt a passive attitude towards the world. Motor competence and manipulation, by means of which the individual explores the world for himself, are not encouraged. The child's personal desires and intentions, which might differentiate him from others, are not emphasized. What matters for them is the child's conformity to the group. Thus their concept of a child is of a being who starts off full of personal desire and intention, but who has increasingly to subordinate such desires to the group. He thus becomes less and less of an individual because he is discouraged from thinking of himself as one. In cultures such as these, therefore, there is no encouragement for the individual to explore the world 'for himself' and find out what is true. What is true is what the group, or the authority figure in the group, says.[1]

We are, of course, familiar with this phenomenon in a less thoroughgoing form; for the appeal to the authority of the leader, parent, teacher or group and the discouragement of individual testing out is one of the main characteristics both of the second main developmental stage in the Piaget-Kohlberg theory and of traditionalist and collectivist types of society. But this attitude towards rules is not just the product of vague social pressure and expectations; it is also produced and perpetuated by the conscious techniques which we now call 'indoctrination'. For 'indoctrination' involves the passing on of fixed beliefs in a way which discourages questions about their validity. Societies, like the USSR in which indoctrination is widespread, are not necessarily societies in which reasoning is altogether discouraged. What is discouraged is the questioning of the *validity* of moral and political beliefs and the placing of any emphasis on the role of the individual in determining his own destiny. They thus allow plenty

[1] See P. M. Greenfield and J. S. Bruner, 'Culture and cognitive growth', in D. A. Goslin, *Handbook of Socialization: Theory and Research* (Chicago: Rand McNally, 1961).

of scope for the attitude to rules which is characteristic of Piaget's second stage but actively discourage any movement towards the autonomous stage, which they regard as an aberration of individualistic societies.

(*c*) *The achievement of autonomy*

So far I have sketched the sorts of social influences and techniques, such as indoctrination, which discourage people from passing beyond the second stage of 'good-boy' morality. What is to be said about the type of influences that encourage development? It is difficult to say much even in a brief space about this because the notion of 'autonomy', which is the dominant feature of the third stage, is itself very complex.

There is, first of all, the notion of authenticity or genuineness. The suggestion is that a person accepts rules for himself, that his activities are not just those that he indulges in because they are the done thing, that his emotional responses are not simply second-hand. Negatively this suggests that he is not just motivated by approval or disapproval from the peer-group or from authority figures. More positively it suggests that there must be some feature of a course of conduct, or of a situation which he appraises, which constitutes a non-artificial reason for his decision or judgment, as distinct from extrinsic associations provided by praise and blame, reward and punishment, and so on, which are artificially created by the demands of others.

Second, there is the aspect of autonomy stressed by Kant and Piaget—the ability to stand and reflect on rules, activities and emotional responses and to subject them to criticism from the point of view of their validity and appropriateness.

Third, there is the suggestion of integrity and strength of will, the ability to stick to a judgment or course of conduct in the face of counter-inclinations. These counter-inclinations often derive from motivations which consolidate conformity at previous stages—for example, fear of punishment, disapproval and ostracism.

How, then, are these different aspects of autonomy developed? A general preliminary point must be made which is that we cannot expect young people to manage on their own unless they are given concrete opportunities to do so. This thought presumably lies behind the 'Outward Bound' movement and the public schools system of prefects. But such opportunities must be realistically related to responsibilities which it is reasonable for people to take. If too open a situation is created we are likely to get relapses back to and embeddedness in the second stage of morality due to the fear of freedom about which Eric Fromm has written so eloquently.[1]

This conditional encouragement of the individual to strike out on his own is particularly important in the development of authenticity. There is a strange misconception that haunts the Socratic insistence that we should discover what we really want, which is that we

[1] See E. Fromm, *The Fear of Freedom* (London: Routledge & Kegan Paul, 1942).

can come to understand this before we actually try things out. But the truth is that we often only come to know what we genuinely want or feel *by* trying things out. And surely, behind this demand lies the insistence on the importance of truth which is inseparable from the Socratic care of the soul. As E. M. Forster put it, through one of his characters:[1]

> Take an old man's word for it: there's nothing worse than a muddle in all the world. It is easy to face death and fate, and the things that sound so dreadful. It is on my muddles that I look back with horror—on the things that I might have avoided. We can help one another but little. I used to think I could teach people the whole of life, but I know better now, and all my teaching of George has come down to this: beware of muddle.

For the second aspect of autonomy to develop, namely critical reflection on rules, two conditions must be operative. First, the individual has to be sensitive to considerations which are to act as principles to back rules—for example, to the suffering of others. Second, he has to be able, by reasoning, to view such considerations as reasons for doing some things rather than others. How individuals develop the required sensitivity is largely a matter of speculation, to which I have already referred in my comments about the origins and development of the humanistic conscience. What, then, can be done about encouraging the development of reasoning of this sort so that rules have the backing

[1] E. M. Forster, *A Room with a View* (Harmondsworth: Penguin Books, 1935), pp. 214–15.

of principles? Presumably, reasons for doing things can be indicated quite early on, even though it is appreciated that the child cannot yet think in this way. For unless there is this kind of 'cognitive stimulation' in the environment it is improbable that the child will emerge to the autonomous stage. Obviously an atmosphere of discussion and debating especially amongst children who are a bit older, will help to stimulate this development. Language, too, which approximates to what Bernstein calls an 'elaborated code', is very important in aiding this development as well as non-arbitrary methods of teaching rules.[1] I am not saying, of course, that any sane parent or teacher will, in the early stages, make a child's acceptance of the reasons a condition for his doing what is sensible. All I am saying is that rules can be presented in a non-arbitrary way *before* children are capable of accepting them for the reasons given, to help them to get to the stage when they follow rules *because of* the reasons for them. But it does not follow from this that, on many occasions, parents and teachers may not have to insist on certain forms of conduct even though the children do not accept the good sense of it.

There is little to say about the development of the third aspect of autonomy, which is connected with strength of will, because so little is known about it. My

[1] B. B. Bernstein, 'Social class and linguistic development: a theory of social learning', in A. H. Halsey, J. Floud, and C. A. Anderson, *Education, Economy and Society* (New York: The Free Press, 1961).

guess is that habit-training is not unimportant because virtues such as courage, determination and integrity, have to be exercised in the face of counter-inclinations. Unless a boy has some training in acting in the face of fear or anxiety it seems probable that he will be overwhelmed by them if he encounters them at a later stage when attempting to take a line of his own. This was manifestly the assumption of educators in the public school tradition who believed in some kind of transfer of training in this sphere. They tended, however, to stress too much the negative side of 'strength of will', the schooling of individuals to resist fear and temptation. They neglected, perhaps, the sensitization to positive considerations which give point to the exercise of will. It is not helpful to exhort a boy to show courage at football, and to shame him if he is cowardly, when he can see no point in football and would much rather be spending his time in some other way.

Attention has been drawn to positive motivations in the spheres both of authenticity and of strength of will. But they are equally important in the development of reasoning. How is the concern for truth developed, which lies behind both authenticity and any kind of reasoning, which is not a mere shadow-play? It may well be that its basis is in curiosity which is innate. But there is ample evidence to suggest that curiosity can be quickly stamped out or damped down by social discouragement—witness some of the children in our primary schools. Also, curiosity is too sporadic and capricious in its operation to provide in itself the stable sort of motivation that is required. It is only when curiosity is supported by and encased in a social tradition, such as that of science, which insists that truth matters, that a form of motivation emerges that is capable of supporting the ideal of autonomy. When children's curiosity leads them to disciplines such as science it becomes more precisely articulated in what I have called the rational passions.[1] And these passions begin to get a grip when children participate in enquiries with experienced people whose hatred of arbitrariness and irrelevance, whose concern for clarity and coherence, and whose determination to look at the facts and to subject every assumption to criticism, is conveyed to others. In a similar way the generalized desire for mastery passes into more precise forms of getting things right. In brief, although there may be some kind of 'natural' spark for the passions which lies at the heart of reason, they are fanned into a steady flame by the various disciplines into which reason has become differentiated. And these disciplines are social traditions into which children have laboriously to be initiated.

These disciplines of thought do not simply provide motivational channels along which the concern for truth can flow; they also provide the equipment which is necessary for any individual to make up his mind in an informed and imaginative way about the alternatives open to him. To demand that people should decide

[1] See R. S. Peters, 'Reason and passion', in G. Vesey (ed.), *The Proper Study*, Royal Institute of Philosophy Lectures, vol. 2, 1969–70 (London: Macmillan, 1971).

things for themselves if they have been provided with no conceptual equipment to explore and weigh up the alternatives is a fatuous type of fraud. They must have some breadth of content in order to be provided with concrete samples of the sorts of things between which they must choose; they must also study some of the forms of experience which have a special position in informing their choice. By this I mean studies such as literature, history, religion and social sciences which, if imaginatively entered into, enlarge their perspective of the predicament of man and so put their choice in a less abstract setting. In the development of autonomy, first-hand experiment is essential. But it must be informed and sensitized by initiation into those imaginative explorations which are part of our cultural heritage as civilized men.

3 THE INFLUENCE OF INSTITUTIONS

So far I have been making suggestions about the ways in which individuals such as parents and teachers can wittingly or unwittingly provide appropriate forms of 'cognitive stimulation' which help the development of a rational form of life. Nothing has been said about the all-pervasive influence of institutions which provide a potent source of latent learning for the growing child. Of particular significance is the general control system of the school and the motivational assumptions which support it. For Piaget's and Kohlberg's stages of development are 'writ large' in these all-pervasive features of the institution. It is unlikely that autonomy will be much encouraged by an authoritarian system of control in which anything of importance is decided by the fiat of the headmaster and in which the prevailing assumption is that the appeal to a man is the only method of determining what is correct. Similarly, in the motivational sphere students are unlikely to develop a delight in doing things for reasons intrinsic to them if rewards and punishment, meted out both by the staff and by a fierce examination system, provide the stable incentives to the discipline of learning; for the institution itself embodies an attitude to conduct which is appropriate to Piaget's first stage of development. These institutional realities are bound to structure the perceptions of the students. If an institution embodies only an attitude to rules that is characteristic of an earlier stage of development, teachers who attempt to encourage a more developed attitude have an uphill task; for in their attempts at 'cognitive stimulation' they are working against the deadening directives of the institution.

The inference to be drawn from this is not that every school which upholds an ideal of autonomy should straightaway abolish its punishment and examination systems and introduce a school parliament which should direct the affairs of the institution in a way which is acceptable to autonomous men. Apart from the rational objections to the possibility of educational institutions being purely 'democratic'[1] it

[1] See P. H. Hirst and R. S. Peters, *The Logic of Education* (London: Routledge & Kegan Paul, 1970), ch. 7.

ignores the implications to be drawn from the Piaget-Kohlberg theory. For children have to pass from seeing rules as connected with punishments and rewards to seeing them as ways of maintaining a gang-given or authoritatively ordained rule-structure before they can adopt a more autonomous attitude towards them. Kohlberg has shown that many adolescents are still only at the first 'pre-moral' stage, so the suggestion that an institution should be devised for them which is structured only in terms of the final stage is grossly inappropriate. Progressive schools, therefore, which insist *from the start* on children learning only what interests them, on making their own decisions and running their own affairs, ignore the crucial role which the stage of conventional morality plays in moral development. The more enlightened ones in fact have a firm authority structure for the school which is arranged so that increasing areas of discretion and participation in decision making are opened up for the older pupils.

It must, finally, be stressed that, though there are stages in character-development, which are 'writ-large' in systems of institutional control, the arrangement is a hierarchical one. Earlier stages are not completely superseded; rather they are, ideally speaking, caught up in and transformed by the next stage. When a system maintained purely by naked force and the dispensation of rewards gives way to a system dependent on the belief in the sanctity of rules enshrined in tradition or laid down by authority, force and rewards are not abandoned. Rather, they are placed in the background as palpable supports for the authority structure. Similarly, when traditional systems are challenged, authority becomes rationalized, not superseded. Its structure is adapted to the reasons for having it. But the insistence that a rule is a rule, which is so characteristic of the second stage, persists.

In a similar way the autonomous man is not a person who operates only at the level of a principled morality. He is not impervious to the promise of reward and punishment; he does many things because it is the decent thing to do or because they have been laid down by authority; but he is capable both of doing the same things because he sees their point as flowing from his fundamental principles, and of challenging certain forms of conduct that are laid down and acting differently because of his own convictions. He has, in other words, a rational attitude both to tradition and to authority; but he also carries with him, from the second stage, a firm basis of rules together with an understanding 'from the inside' of what it is to follow a rule.

4 LEARNING THE CONTENT OF MORALITY

What, then, is to be said about learning the *content* of morality; for I have so far been concerned only with the learning of its form and have been stressing the role of various social influences in promoting what Kohlberg calls 'cognitive stimulation'. There are at least three questions which demand an answer. First, is the learning of a content necessary in moral education? Could not children just develop a form of thinking which enables them to work out a content for themselves? Second, if it is, what should this content be? Third, *how* should it be learnt if development of the form of morality is to be encouraged and the 'paradox of moral education' rendered less of a paradox?

(*a*) *Why worry about content?*

There is a kind of abstractness and unreality about the approach to moral education which places exclusive emphasis on the development of a rational form of morality and which considers its content unimportant, dismissing it, as Kohlberg does, as merely 'a bag of virtues'. To start with, even at an early age, children are capable of doing both themselves and others a lot of damage. Hobbes once noted a sobering feature of the human condition which is that a man can be killed by a small child while he is asleep. Also the hazards to small children in modern industrial society are innumerable. So, for reasons both of social security and self-preservation, small children must be taught a basic code which, when internalized, will regulate their behaviour to a certain extent when they are not being supervized. There is also the point that a great number of people do not develop to a rational level of morality. For obvious social reasons, therefore, if the morality of such people is to be unthinking, its content is of crucial importance. If the ordinary citizen is woken up in the night by noises indicating that his house is being burgled, how the thief views rules about property is of academic interest to him. He can hear the clink of his silver as it is being shovelled into a sack in the living room.

But even if the issue is the development of children rather than the more palpable facets of social behaviour there are logical absurdities about any cavalier disregard for content. In the first place, even in the limited area of rule following, which is connected with the exercise of character traits (see Lecture 1, section 2), it is difficult to understand how a person could come to follow rules autonomously if he had not learnt, from the inside, as it were, what it is to follow a rule. And children learn this, presumably, by generalizing their experience of picking up some particular 'bag of virtues'.

In the second place, how is the exercise of a principled form of morality to be conceived without reference to a determinate content? Respect for persons, for instance, is only intelligible in the context of a life in which people occupy roles, take part in activities and enjoy personal relationships. It suggests that people should not be treated just as the occupants of roles, that they should not be judged just for their competence in activities, and that, in more personal relationships, they should not be used just as means to the purposes of others. Such a principle, in other words, sensitizes the individual to the way in which he should conduct himself in the various areas of the moral life (see Lecture 1, section 2) which constitute its content. It could not operate without such a concrete content. Indeed, by calling something like respect for persons a 'principle' we mean that it embodies a consideration to which appeal is made when criticizing, justifying or explaining some determinate content of behaviour or belief.

Usually a principle such as considering people's interests is appealed to in criticism or justification of a social practice such as punishment. But it can also be regarded as a τέλος immanent in roles and social practices. For parents, for instance, considering children's interests is one of the rationales underlying their role: indeed, their role largely defines what this principle *means* in their dealings with their children. Most Utilitarians, too, have stressed the importance of Mill's 'secondary principles' in morality. The Utilitarian, Mill argued, has not to be constantly weighing up the effects of his actions on people's interests any more than a Christian has to thumb through the Bible every time before he acts. The experience of a society with regard to the tendencies of actions in relation to people's interests lies behind its roles and rules. In a similar way concern for truth is to be conceived of as a τέλος underlying the procedures of science. If people practising activities and occupying roles are sensitive to such underlying principles they will adapt their behaviour sensitively to changes in circumstances. If, on the other hand, they are hide-bound traditionalists they may insist on conformity to the minutiae of a code that no longer have any point. Their insensitivity to considerations underlying rules, roles and practices may generate pedantry, scholasticism and bigotry. The

letter of the law matters more to them than its spirit.
(*b*) *What type of content?*
Given then the indispensability of some kind of content for moral education the second question arises
about the type of content which should constitute the
basis of moral education. There is, as a matter of fact, a
kind of unreality about this question if it is framed in
too general a way. For willy-nilly, adults will in fact
introduce children in some way or other to the type of
content which seems to them important. The world
which the child has to inhabit is largely a social world
structured by the roles, rules, activities and relationships
of his parents. He will only become at home in this
world if he makes it his own by internalization. For in
learning to behave as a human being he is, *ipso facto*,
being initiated into the concepts, rules and assumptions
without which he could make no sense of the life of
others. If he is to be viable at all as a human being,
therefore, he has to structure his consciousness with
the microcosm of social life which he encounters in the
home, which will be shot through with the morality of
his parents. The question, therefore, is which elements
of this content are to be *emphasized* by parents. For the
child will be exposed to it *in toto* and will pick much of
it up by imitation and identification whatever their
more explicit child-rearing techniques.

If parents subscribe to some form of the rational
morality outlined in the first lecture they will obviously
emphasize, as soon as the child is ready, those considerations which are later to function as principles in a

rational morality—for example, fairness and consideration for others. They will also emphasize what I previously termed 'basic rules' (see p. 13) such as those to do with contracts and property which can be defended as necessary to the continuance of any tolerable form of social life. What else could they rationally contemplate doing? For they could not hold that there were strong grounds for insisting on at least this minimum content of rules, under any conditions of social life and, at the same time, decline to insist on such rules in their own home.

(c) How teach content?

The more interesting and controversial question is the third question relating to the manner rather than to the matter of early moral education. For how are they to emphasize these rudiments of morality? The obvious answer, it might be thought, is by any method which is meaningful to the child at the stage of development at which he is. In moral education, surely, as in any other form of education, parents and teachers should begin where children are. This is obvious enough; but what it implies for moral learning is not obvious without more detailed analysis of the situation. To simplify these general points I will concentrate on the area of content that is concerned with the learning of rules.

First, there is learning and learning. A rule could just be learnt as a bit of verbalism without any real understanding of its application. But obviously, because the function of moral rules is to regulate people's behaviour rather than just to act as incantations, a child must learn them in the sense of being able to apply them to a variety of situations. This means that he must attend to the situations and to the similarities in them picked out by the rule. Now many things can be learnt just by watching others—for instance, simple skills and reactions to situations. But moral rules could not be learnt just by a mixture of trial and error and watching what others do. For if a child sees his father returning a garden-roller that he has borrowed from next door, there is a problem about recognizing, from the outside, what he is doing. For this series of movements to be recognized as a case of returning what has been borrowed, the child has to understand a complicated network of concepts which structure social life. He could not learn what 'borrowing', as distinct from 'stealing', is without a considerable amount of instruction and explanation. He has to be able to distinguish himself from others, to have notions defining what is 'his' and what belongs to others, to be able to distinguish 'lending' from 'giving', and so on. Parents often punish children for what they call 'stealing'. But the child may not have developed the concepts which enable him to discriminate what he is doing as a case of 'stealing'.

It is inconceivable, for this reason too, that a child could learn to behave morally purely by some process of conditioning in the strict sense. He could not learn not to steal simply by some process of positive reinforcement; for he has to develop the concepts necessary to grasping *what* behaviour is being reinforced. This requires instruction, explanation and other teaching methods by means of which *content* is marked out. Aids to learning, such as reinforcement, should not be confused with processes of learning. Nevertheless, at the early stages of moral learning, aids to learning, which are developments of conditioning such as rewards and punishments, praise and blame, are extremely important. Indeed, Piagetians claim, as has already been explained, that very small children can only see rules first of all as things to be done to avoid punishment or to obtain rewards, and then as forms of behaviour that are approved of or disapproved of by peers and authority figures. In the case of moral learning the importance of such extrinsic aids is not difficult to understand. For a child has not just got to learn how to apply concepts correctly; he has also to learn to behave consistently in the required way. Rules must regulate something and what they regulate are human inclinations. Children have, therefore, to start off their moral life with some kind of habit training. They may come to delight, at the second 'transcendental' stage of morality, in following rules; but often they do not do this because their counter-inclinations are strong. They want something now or they want something at other people's expense. Therefore insistence by parents on rules often has to be backed by extrinsic aids such as rewards and approval in order to provide positive incentives to outweigh the pull of the child's inclinations. And so simple habits are built up.

Parents, therefore, at these early stages have the

option of supplementing example and instruction by the positive extrinsic aids of rewards or approval or by the negative ones of punishment and disapproval. There is strong evidence from psychological research which suggests that the positive aids are much more conducive to moral learning. There is also strong evidence for the efficacy of what psychologists call 'induction'—that is, the process of explaining the rule in the context to which it applies, pointing to consequences of behaviour, and so on.[1] The reasons for this can be related to the logic of the learning situation. If the child is going to learn, in the sense explained, he has to attend to the features of the situation, understand its point of similarity with other situations, and what his actions are likely to bring about. 'Induction' covers the various processes of getting the child to attend to the relevant features of the situation. But, as is well known, attention is difficult to sustain in conditions of anxiety and stress or when the child lacks confidence in his ability to understand. The hypothesis is that punitive and rejecting techniques militate against attention, and hence against learning, by producing anxiety, and undermine the child's confidence in himself. This explains, too, the lack of correlation between love-withdrawal and moral learning. For anxiety is produced by making the keeping of a mother's love contingent upon learning what 'being a

[1] For an excellent survey of evidence see M. L. Hoffman, 'Moral development', in P. H. Mussen (ed.), *Carmichael's Manual of Child Psychology* (New York: Wiley, 1970).

good boy' amounts to. Approval, on the other hand, together with parental warmth, which correlate well with moral learning, are thought to provide incentives for learning in a climate which is not fraught with anxiety.

5 TEACHING CONTENT IN RELATION TO THE DEVELOPMENT OF FORM

The use of such techniques has been considered so far on the assumption that what is being learnt is some content of morality. But an equally important way of looking at them is from the point of whether they aid or hinder the development of the rational form of morality. In this the validity of rules can be questioned and reasons for them discerned which fall under principles as distinct from their artificial associative connection with rewards and punishment, approval and disapproval. Obviously the use of induction is the most appropriate technique in so far as it involves, for example, drawing attention to the consequences for others of a child's actions. But early on this type of technique makes little difference; for it is only when a child is capable of reversibility in thought and can look at actions from the point of view of others that this technique is effective. There are, understandably enough, no consistent findings relating to the effectiveness of induction in promoting moral development until after the pre-school years.[1] 'Induction', in the sense of teaching children rules, will obviously be

[1] See M. L. Hoffman, op.cit., p. 325.

effective. But in so far as it is concerned with trying to indicate to children the reasons for rules it will only be effective when they have reached the appropriate level of cognitive development.

The extrinsic aids to instruction and example, which were discussed in the context of the learning of content, are also extremely relevant when the way content is learnt is considered from the point of view of whether this learning situation is likely or not to promote a rational form of morality later on. It could well be, for instance, that many of the cases studied by psychologists of the Freudian school, of people who become fixated at an early stage of moral development with extreme irrational feelings of guilt and unworthiness about their conduct, are the victims of punitive and rejecting parental techniques. If children are to develop sensibly towards an autonomous form of morality they require a consistent pattern of rules in their early years, backed up by approval for learning. Interestingly enough though, there is evidence to suggest that what Hoffman calls 'humanistic-flexible' individuals do emerge from homes in which parents, though relying on induction and approval, occasionally blow up and use power-assertive techniques.[1] This is quite different from the indiscriminate or systematic use of punishment. On occasions some assertion of power may be necessary for the voice of reason to be heard! Perhaps, too, there is some support for the wry advice that one should never strike a child save in anger!

[1] See M. L. Hoffman, op. cit., p. 340.

Development is also likely to be stunted by complete permissiveness whether this involves inconsistency in relation to what is expected or no determinate expectations; for the anxiety created by such inconsistency or anomie is not conducive to learning. Also, under such conditions the child has little basis for predictability in his social environment which is necessary for anticipating consequences of actions. A predictable type of environment, on the other hand, together with an accepting attitude towards the child, provide conditions under which he can be secure and be disposed gradually to adopt a more reflective attitude towards rules. His confidence in the future and his trust in people is not undermined and he does not develop a negative self-picture. In this sort of atmosphere standards can be pointed out and insisted on, but not in a way which humiliates the child and diminishes his view of himself as a person. For people's conception of themselves, and their view of what it is possible for them to become, depends enormously on the messages about themselves that they read off from other people's expectations of them.

6 THE CHARGE OF INAUTHENTICITY

It might be objected that this willingness to use extrinsic aids such as rewards and approval is rather deplorable. It may not have disastrous consequences like the fierce use of punishment or disapproval. But even if no explicit attempt is made, as in indoctrination, to keep the individual at a conformist level of morality, will it not tend to ingrain in the individual a second-hand instrumental view of life? Will his moral life not be one of 'toil', lacking in authenticity? Would it not be better to rely on the more intrinsic motivations of delight in the mastery of rules and in the spontaneous co-operation exemplified by peer-groups at play? Is not the content of morality more effectively picked up in these more spontaneous situations from older members of the peer-group?

There is point in this criticism, but it represents altogether too idealistic a picture of what the situation actually is in peer-group co-operation. Certainly these intrinsic types of motivation exist, and are very important at the second stage of development. Certainly children learn much from others who are just a bit more advanced than they are—as the experiments of Turiel have shown.[1] But the pressure of social approval and disapproval is very strong in such situations. Indeed, disapproval for the unwilling or the incompetent is probably stronger than approval for the conformist. Also, if an individual wishes to go his own way and to stand out against what is laid down by his peers, his situation is a parlous one unless there is some other source of approval, emanating from adults, which will support him in his strivings for independence.

The use of approval is surely on a par with the

---

[1] E. Turiel, 'Developmental processes in the child's moral thinking', in P. H. Mussen, J. Langer, M. Covington (eds), *Trends and Issues in Developmental Psychology* (New York: Holt, Rinehart & Winston, 1969).

mechanism of identification with adults which is equally important in transmitting moral content at this stage. It depends on whether or not it is regarded as a transitional device. If a teacher finds that a pupil admires him and tends to copy him and to adopt his values, he can either perpetuate this stage or try to use this admiration to turn the pupil's attention to features which are intrinsic to the activities or forms of conduct to which he is committed. He can use the admiration felt for him to aid cognitive stimulation and the development of authenticity and first-hand appreciation. Or he can revel in the feeling of power that this situation gives him and do nothing to move the pupil's attention away from him, towards the form of life into which he is trying to initiate him.

There is no evidence to suggest that this affectively changed link between the generations necessarily inhibits the development of autonomy. It depends entirely on how it is handled. The wise use of authority does not necessitate being authoritarian. For the authoritarian is the person who not only delights in laying down the law; he also constantly appeals to his status or peculiar insight as its source. 'I'm your father and I'm telling you that you ought not to smoke' is the pattern of his directives. He does not appeal to the publicly available reasons for refraining from smoking. The question, too, has to be faced: what else is practicable? If children in their early years cannot acquire rules because they see the proper point in them and if, for the reasons explained, they have to start off with some 'bag of virtues', it is difficult to see what other alternatives are open. If they can think in no other way about rules at this early stage, it is difficult to make the charge of inauthenticity stick. For there exists no possibility of authenticity. Also for some virtues, such as fairness and concern for others, it is difficult to see what further reasons could be given. For sensitivity to them is a precondition of there being reasons. For as principles they determine relevance for reasoning in morals.

It should be stressed, however, that this early combination of 'induction' and positive 'reinforcement' does not constitute indoctrination; for 'indoctrination' picks out a special manner of instruction. It consists in getting children to accept a fixed body of rules by the use of techniques which incapacitate them from adopting a critical autonomous attitude towards them. Children are permanently fixated with a 'good-boy' type of morality. They are perhaps led to associate obedience to such a fixed body of rules with loyalty to their group or to some authority figure whose disapproval they dare not incur. The shaming techniques of the traditional English public school or of a communist collective are an example of this. But not all instruction need employ such indoctrinating techniques. Indeed, it must not employ them if development towards a rational type of morality is to occur.

The crucial problem of methods in early moral education can, therefore, be stated in this way: given that it is thought desirable that children should develop an autonomous form of morality, and given that, if Piaget and Kohlberg are right, they cannot, in their early years, learn in a way that presupposes such an autonomous form, how can a basic content for morality be provided that gives them a firm basis for moral behaviour without impeding the development of a rational form of it? What non-rational methods of teaching aid, or at least do not impede, the development of rationality?

It is to this complex problem of instruction that sensitive parents and teachers should address themselves instead of withdrawing from the scene for fear of indoctrination. For by withdrawing and refusing to act as models and instructors they are equally in danger of impeding the development towards autonomy that they desire. It is indeed significant that Bronfenbrenner singles out the weakening of links between the generations, with the consequent lessening of opportunities for modelling and identification, as the main cause-factor in 'the Unmaking of the American Child'. 'Children', he says 'used to be brought up by their parents'.[1]

[1] U. Bronfenbrenner, *Two Worlds of Childhood* (London: Allen & Unwin, 1971).

Lecture Three

REASON, PASSION AND
LEVELS OF LIFE

INTRODUCTION

IN my first lecture I developed the theme that the complex content of the moral life can be unified, to a certain extent, by a form in which reason and compassion can be combined with varying degrees of emphasis. In this lecture I want to say more about this form of life, especially in respect to the role of reason in it. I want to attack the common assumption that the use of reason is a passionless business, the prerogative perhaps of the unfeeling or the middle-aged. I want to argue that the antithesis between reason and passion is misconceived. The proper contrast is between levels of life, each characterized by distinctive levels of thought and feeling. Those who demand instant gratification, who cultivate violence or mystical experience, or who merely do what others do, are all certainly resisting the claims of reason on them. But what they are resisting is not just the demand that they should reflect and calculate; it is also the influence of passions that underlie a level of life.

Reason and Compassion

Hume, I suppose, was the hero of my first lecture in that he put forward a view of virtue which did justice to its complexity; but he is the villain of this lecture in that he made explicit a view of the relationship between reason and passion which is both widespread and wrong-headed. He claimed that reason is merely the *ability* to make inductive and deductive inferences. He contrasted reason, which is inert, with passions which he regarded as psychological entities which move people to act. He did, however, draw attention to a special class of 'disinterested passions' which, because of their calmness and steadiness, are often mistaken for reason. He had in mind the attitudes which go with taking the point of view of the impartial spectator. Hume did not appreciate, however, that these so-called passions are intimately connected with the use of reason rather than distinct entities that are liable to be mistaken for it; for the use of reason is inexplicable without them. He also took too limited a view of them; for the ones which he mentioned, I shall argue, are just particular examples of a wider class of passions which I shall call the 'rational passions'. Calmness, too, is not always a feature of them. When Bertrand Russell was called 'the passionate sceptic' the suggestion was that his passion for truth was anything but calm.

It would be possible, I suppose, using the example of Russell, to make the case for the passionate aspect of reason very briefly. It could be noted that anyone who is committed to the use of reason must care about the point of its use. In other words, he must care about finding out how things are, about getting things right, about tracking down what is the case. Russell manifestly had such feelings in a very highly developed form; for he accused pragmatists of cosmic impiety in supposing that the justification for holding on to beliefs depends, in the end, on their satisfactoriness for the forwarding of human purposes. But, I think, it is more interesting and instructive to dissect in more detail the anatomy of reason and to point to the passions that are connected with each sphere of its functioning.

The most general feature of the use of reason is the transcendence of the here and now by the use of generalizations, plans and rules in making inferences. This enlargement of the context of life is supported by various passions. First, there is love of system, classification and order, to which children become most prone at what Piaget calls the stage of concrete operations. This love of order was prominent in Plato's account of reason. Freud also regarded it as one of the main affective sources of civilization. It can, of course, get out of hand as in some metaphysical systems when a form of order is forced on resistant material. Superficial similarities are stressed at the expense of palpable differences. In practical affairs, too, intellectuals are very prone to excesses of this sort. A plan or formula is dreamed up and the attempt is made to slot individuals into it, without due regard for their differences.

Second, there are passions which oppose lapses in

the use of generalizations and rules. There is, for instance, the hatred of contradictions and inconsistencies, together with the love of clarity and hatred of confusion without which words could not be held to relatively constant meanings and testable rules and generalizations stated. A reasonable man cannot, without some special explanation, slap his sides with delight or express indifference if he is told that what he says is confused, incoherent and perhaps riddled with contradictions. Then, third, there are a group of passions that go with the antipathy between reason and the appeal to the particular. The use of reason is usually contrasted with the appeal to authority, revelation and tradition. These appeals are all particular examples of something more general, namely the settling of what is at issue by the appeal to some particular man, body, or set of practices rather than by an appeal to general considerations. A more formal way of making this point is to say that in the use of reason particularities of time, place and identity are irrelevant to the determination of what is true, correct, or to be done. In science, for instance, which is a paradigm case of reason in action, appeal is made to a universal law which anyone can test. Nothing ultimately depends on the identity of the individual who states or tests it. Similarly, in practical conduct, when one says 'No' to oneself, there is a presupposition that, other things being equal, the mere position in time of the satisfaction of the desire is irrelevant. This is a point well made by Sidgwick in his axiom of prudence, that 'Hereafter *as such* is to be regarded neither more nor less than now.'[1] There is also Mabbott's emphasis on the use of reason in devising time-schedules for the satisfaction of desire, which is a device for avoiding conflict.[2] This presupposes that, other things being equal, mere position in time of a desire's satisfaction is an irrelevant consideration. The same sort of point can be made about identity in cases where there is reasoning about the distribution of something good. If I or you are going to benefit, some special characterization of me or you has to be given which relevantly differentiates us from others, if the fact that it is I or you that is going to benefit is to be accorded any special significance. This abstract principle of no distinctions without relevant differences is central to all forms of reasoning. Reason, in other words, is the antithesis of arbitrariness. In its operation it is supported by the appropriate passions which are mainly negative in character—the hatred of irrelevance, special pleading and arbitrary fiat. The more developed emotion of indignation is aroused when some excess of arbitrariness is perpetrated in a situation where people's interests and claims are at stake. The positive side of this is the passion for fairness and impartial consideration of claims.

The irreconcilability of the use of reason with ego-centricity and arbitrariness is a reflection of its essenti-

[1] H. Sidgwick, *The Methods of Ethics* (London: Macmillan, 1962), p. 381.
[2] J. Mabbott, 'Reason and desire', *Philosophy*, xxxviii, April 1953, 114–15.

ally public character. It is public not just in the sense that its vehicle is language whose concepts and rules of syntax are a public possession, but in the further sense that, even when it takes place in the individual's head, it is an internalization of public procedures—those of criticism, the production of counter-examples and the suggestion of different points of view. Of course, reason, in this developed sense, has its origin in the primitive operations associated with the use of intelligence—the adjustment of expectations in the light of discrepant situations. But in reasoning proper, this caution born of the frequent experience of being in error becomes the explicit principle, enunciated by Francis Bacon, that a search must always be made for the negative instance. Conscious, explicit attempts must be made to falsify assumptions, to find exceptions to rules; for only in this way can a body of reliable assumptions and rules be built. There must, also, be some form of public test to decide between competing assumptions. This means not just agreement about how answers are to be sought but also about the types of considerations that are to count as deciding between possible answers. Indeed, without such agreement in judgments for the application of concepts to situations there are problems about the meaningfulness of statements, let alone about their testability.

There is no time to explore the difficulties and differences connected with objectivity in the different spheres of reasoning, with objectivity in science, mathematics, law, morals and interpretations of other people's behaviour. My concern in this lecture is only to point to the distinctive passions that make it possible. There is, first of all, the determination to get to the bottom of things, to find out what really is the case, what the correct interpretation is or what the right thing to do or think is. Linked with this is the feeling of humility which is necessary to the whole-hearted acceptance of the possibility that one may be in error. A man who is prepared to reason must feel strongly that he must follow the arguments and decide things in terms of where they lead. He must have a sense of the givenness, of the impersonality of such considerations. In so far as thoughts about persons enter his head they should be tinged with the respect which is due to another who, like himself, may have a point of view which is worth considering, who may have a glimmering of the truth which has so far eluded himself. A person who proceeds in this way, who is influenced by such passions, is what we call a reasonable man. He decides in the light of the best evidence available and listens to what other people say. In moral situations he takes account of the claims of others instead of riding roughshod over them. The unreasonable man, on the other hand, makes up his mind on the basis of inadequate evidence. He is a victim of prejudice and ego-centricity. He is biased and short-sighted and, because he seldom listens to what others say and lacks sensitivity to their claims, he is obtuse, wilful, arbitrary and pigheaded.

So much, then, for the types of passion that are

indispensable to the use of reason. The disinterestedness of Hume's impartial spectator has been shown to figure amongst them. But Hume thought that this type of passion was distinct from reason. At best it could be mistaken for reason, instead of being conceptually linked with its operation. This was not just because he had a narrow view of 'reason', equating it just with the ability to make inductive and deductive inferences without exploring what even this presupposed. It was also because he thought that passions were 'discrete existences' that could exist, as it were, cut off from other features of mental life. It is this assumption about his concept of 'passion' that must now be examined.

2 THE RATIONALITY OF PASSION

Hume, as a matter of fact, used 'passion' in rather a technical, philosophical sense, to speak of a state of mind such as fear or benevolence that moves people to act. Our ordinary use of 'passion', however, is more closely connected with its etymology, with the suggestion that we are in a state of mind in respect of which we are, as it were, sufferers. Something has come over us. Whether or not we are disposed to act, as a consequence, or whether we are just struck in a heap is a further question. In order, however, to allow for both possibilities, and in order to avoid such ambiguities connected with the use of the word 'passion', I shall use more specific terms such as 'emotion' and 'motive'.

The basic, and perhaps paradoxical point that I wish to make about 'emotions' and 'motives' is that, although manifestly these terms relate in some way to our feelings, they are also intimately connected with cognition, that is, with our ways of understanding situations. States of mind, such as envy, pity, fear and remorse, which we would be prepared to call 'emotions' and 'motives', are distinguishable from each other mainly because they are connected with different ways of viewing situations. A man who is envious sees a situation under the aspect of someone else having something that he wants; a man who is afraid sees a situation as dangerous, as threatening his life or security. The 'feeling' aspect of these states of mind is connected with the fact that these ways of viewing situations are not, as it were, a matter of indifference to us. Features are picked out which are of importance to us, which are sources of pain and pleasure, harm and benefit. When such distinctive, feeling-laden thoughts are connected with things that we do, we talk of 'motives'. A person acts out of envy or jealousy. His non-neutral thoughts about someone having something that he wants become connected with a variety of action patterns, the purpose of which is to remedy the situation in some way. When, on the other hand, these thoughts are connected simply with things that come over a man, which may get him into a state or affect his perception, judgment and manner of acting, we speak of such states of mind as 'emotions'.[1] A man may

[1] For further discussion of these points see R. S. Peters, 'Emotions and the category of passivity', *Proc. Aristotelian Soc.*, 1961–2, 117–34; and 'The education of the emotions', in M. Arnold, *Feelings and Emotions* (New York: Academic Press, 1970).

sweat or shiver with fear, boil with anger and blush with embarrassment. His judgment may be warped by jealousy or heightened by fear or joy. We naturally speak of 'emotion' in situations like these in which distinctive types of thoughts are linked with various forms of passivity.

If we think of such states of mind from the point of view of the possible influence of reason on them there are two major respects in which such an influence might operate. On the one hand, it could affect the types of thoughts that a person has; on the other hand, it might influence the type of action which he takes as a result or the form of his expression of emotion. Let us consider these types of influence in turn.

(*a*) *The influence of reason on appraisals of situations*

Suppose that a man is jealous because he thinks that someone is showing undue attention to his wife. There are two respects in which his view of the situation might be held to be unreasonable. First, it might be said that he had no cause to be jealous. In other words, he had got his facts wrong and misinterpreted the situation accordingly. The man, who is being cast in the role of Cassio, is of a friendly disposition. He makes everyone feel as if they are his long-lost friends. There is nothing particular in his attention to the jealous man's wife to give grounds for jealousy. In extreme cases, if there was absolutely nothing in his behaviour that could be construed as justifying the belief that he had seductive thoughts about the wife in question, the husband's reaction might be described as not just unreasonable but as completely irrational.[1] It would be similar to the terror which some people exhibit when confronted with a mouse. Second, however, a more fundamental criticism of a man's jealousy might be mounted. It might be agreed that another man was definitely making progress with his friend's wife. The husband was not misinterpreting the situation. But, it might be said, to be jealous at all is unreasonable, even irrational. For why should anyone think that he had any special claims of this sort on another? Why should he get so steamed up if someone else ventures into what he, in his possessiveness, regards as his special domain? This type of criticism is basically a moral one. It raises doubts of a fundamental sort about conceptions of rights and special relationships that underlie the concept of 'jealousy'. Indeed, in some cases, 'unreasonable' might seem far too weak as a term of condemnation.

There is not time to go through a list of states of mind that are usually thought to be undesirable in order to see whether there is any unitary thread to this type of moral criticism. Manifestly some, such as hatred and malice, are condemned because, in a fairly straightforward way, they exhibit a lack of concern for others. From the point of view of the influence of reason, however, there is another type of condemnation which is more interesting. This is because they

[1] See R. S. Peters, 'Reason and passion', in G. Vesey (ed.), *The Proper Study*, Royal Institute of Philosophy Lectures, vol. 4 (London: Macmillan, 1971).

exhibit an undue preoccupation with self; perhaps, too, a lack of respect for others which goes with the arbitrary assertion of the relentless ego. Pride, lust, jealousy, envy and ambition are in this category, to mention only a few.

Such states of mind give rise to interesting speculations about the basis of the doctrine of original sin. There is an innate, biological basis for some emotions and motives, notably fear and anger. It could be argued, therefore, that in the case of these states of mind only the first type of criticism is appropriate; they can be deemed unreasonable but not vicious. In other words, it could be said that, human nature being what it is, and the conditions of life on earth being what they are, human beings just are going to feel angry and afraid. The only realistic task, therefore, for those who wish to maximize the influence of reason, is to try to ensure that people feel this way in situations which really are threatening or frustrating. The second moral type of criticism is inappropriate because of the truth that lies behind the saying that 'ought implies can'. It is no good saying that it is never appropriate for human beings to feel angry or afraid in any situations if their biological make-up is such that, in *some* form, they will be subject to such feelings. Supposing, however, that theorists like Hobbes and Freud, who stressed *also* the universal and unalterable tendency of human beings to preserve themselves, to think of themselves first and foremost, are right. There would then be a similar sort of inappropriateness in the type of moral criticism which sought to eradicate self-referential states of mind all together. At best it could attempt to harness such feelings to appropriate subjects and to minimize their influence in comparison with self-transcending feelings such as wonder, concern for others, respect and the sense of justice. It would be accepted, for instance, that man just is going to feel some pride. But it would be stressed that it is more important to feel strongly about the ends or standards which he may have had a hand in bringing about or preserving. The sonnet, the bridge, or the abundant harvest is the thing, not a man's cleverness in contriving them. And if, however he is brought up, a man is going to feel some sort of pride, at least he can be encouraged to base it on a realistic assessment of what he has in fact contributed to some project or achievement that really is worthwhile.

There may, then, be considerations which make some types of moral criticism of states of mind inappropriate. Whatever is thought about this issue, however, there will usually be some appropriateness in the first type of criticism in terms of unreasonableness; for such states of mind always imply beliefs about people and situations and these may be mistaken. But to ensure the influence of reason in this sphere is no easy task. For, as Francis Bacon graphically illustrated in his doctrine of the idols, the determination to look at the facts, to care about how things are, goes against an inveterate tendency of the human mind. Our beliefs tend to follow the lines of our wishes and dreads; we rig situations to match our moods. This is particularly evident in our dealings with each other, a sphere in which it is notoriously difficult to be objective, to discern what lies behind people's frowns and hesitations in a way which is not ineradicably self-referential. Indeed, a great deal of human behaviour which, at first glance, seems motivated by malice, hatred and other forms of bloody-mindedness, on closer analysis turns out to be based on forms of misperception which arise from this source. Like Raymond Chandler's hero most people are quiet men going about their own job. But they lack the imagination to realize that others are also in this position. They thus interpret the bank-manager's refusal to grant a small overdraft as personally directed against them. They ignore the logic of his life—the pressures put on him by his superiors. The motorist comes upon cyclists, two abreast, pedalling home in a leisurely way gossiping about the day's events. He swears at them and vows once again that cyclists ought to be taxed. And they, equally pre-occupied with the logic of their own lives, mutter about arrogant 'road-hogs' spreading din and disdain in their wake. To stand back a bit from our own preoccupations, to peer into the logic of other people's lives, is not something that comes easily to human beings. Sporadic curiosity, of course, we may frequently exhibit. But there is a great difference between this and the settled determination to base beliefs on a more objective assessment of the facts. This is surely one of the most important spheres of the influence of reason on the understanding of our situation.

(b) The influence of reason on desire

When a person has passionate thoughts about a situation it is often the case that he also feels moved to *do* something about it. A man, for instance, often acts out of jealousy, jealousy functioning as a motive for him. But this is not always so. In wonder, for instance, what is there to be done? In grief, there may be nothing to be done, which can remedy the situation; so the individual may *express* his emotion, which is rather different from acting out of grief. Sometimes, as in moral indignation, exclamations or expletives may be a substitute for appropriate action. There is certainly, in such situations, a *wish* of some sort that is connected with seeing the situation in a certain light. But the wish contingently may not become a determinate want and, in some cases there may be considerations which make wants, issuing in action patterns, inappropriate. An angry man may just wish that the person who is thwarting him may drop dead, but may have no disposition to bring about this wished-for end himself. A wife, grieving for her dead husband, may wish that he were alive, but what can she actually *do* to bring this end about? She may, of course, *express* how she feels in a more or less coherent form. To study the 'rationality' of such expressions of emotion would really take us into aesthetics, which is beyond the scope of this paper. But at least it can be said that judgments are possible in this sphere. Expressions can be more or less appropriate in a variety of dimensions.

In many cases, however, these indeterminate wishes

issue in action by reaching the level of wants. It is by means of reason that this transformation takes place. First of all the ends wished for come to be conceived in more determinate ways and according to standards definitive of reality thinking. One may wish for the moon; but what could one actually do with it if one had it? Realistic thought about the object brings with it aspects under which it may not be desirable. A child may wish his father dead; but what else does this end bring with it in addition to the absence of a frustrating person? This leads to the distinction between what is wanted and what is *really* wanted. Second, questions about means are introduced. How could one ever get the moon? How can the dead ever be brought to life? There are ends which, in general, it is impossible to achieve. There are also ends which it is impossible for a particular individual to achieve. The tone deaf might wish to be able to play the violin like Menuhin but it is not something that he could realistically want. Conversely, if there is something that he wants, such as to be prime minister, and if he sees that he cannot achieve this end unless he joins a political party, then this is something that he must do. Finally, the individual may be led by reason to see that the pursuit of some end is not compatible with the pursuit of another. It is not easy to combine scholarly research with the hurly-burly of political life. The individual, therefore, may have to make decisions about priorities or impose schedules on his wants. Otherwise he is going to be subject to perpetual conflicts. An irrational man is one who, because he is possessed by some unruly wish, is impervious to the influence of such considerations. He veers towards some end that he does not really want; he is unable to take the steps necessary to bringing about what he wants; he cannot lay aside doing things which he knows will put him in conflict situations which he finds intolerable.

(c) *Reason and 'care'*

These points about the influence of reason are, of course, as old as Plato. So there is little need to elaborate them further. But there is a further point about the connection between reason and the types of end that are worthy of pursuit which is suggested by John Passmore's recent book on *The Perfectibility of Man*.[1] Passmore ends his critique of different forms of perfectibilism with an articulation of three characteristic stances that can be adopted towards human activities and achievements. On the one hand, is the search for unalloyed *enjoyment* without care. The mystic, like the modern hippy, is in search of a condition in which 'there is consciousness of an object in a manner which is devoid of anxiety—a seeing without stirring, without concern, without care' (p. 213). Connections with the past and future are ignored; man's capacities as a generalizing, rational animal are not exercised. This condition, also exhibited by children at play, is one of 'pure activity, without past or future, and freed of worldly pressure and constraints.' On the other hand,

[1] J. Passmore, *The Perfectibility of Man* (London: Duckworth, 1970).

there is the condition of *toil* exhibited by the Puritans and other supporters of the delay of gratification. On this view of life most things have to be done for the sake of some further end. They involve care and anxiety all right; but there is no enjoyment in them. They have to be persisted in to obtain some external end—to earn money, to gain prestige or to fulfil an obligation.

Contrasted with these extreme stances is the 'humane' view of life to which Passmore himself subscribes. This involves care—a wary consciousness of the past and future and of the place of what is being done in the passage through the present. But what is being done is not persisted in purely for the sake of some external end. In the first place there is *enjoyment* in performing well according to the standards required. But such care could be divorced from any concern about the point of the activity. A philosopher, for instance, might enjoy putting forward clever arguments; but the arguments might really not show much of importance in the context of the discussion. A man might enjoy sexual relationships and delight in love as a game; but he might not really care about the woman concerned. A judge might revel in the shrewdness of his judgments but not care whether the effect of them is to bring the law into disrepute. So, in the second place, the humane, civilized attitude requires not simply enjoyment in what is being done according to appropriate standards but an enjoyment that is not adrift from the underlying point of the activity. The scientist must care about truth and his delight in experiments should not be cut adrift from this underlying concern. The civilized life requires, in brief, the transformation of desire by the influence of reason and the rational passions. There must be a lack of egocentricity—a concern for the object of the activity and its standards, and not its debasement which is pride in one's own cleverness. There must be humility towards its givenness, towards the impersonal demands of its standards. And there must be a sense of its connection with other things in life.

3 LEVELS OF LIFE

The significance of these features of what Passmore calls a 'humane' or 'civilized' life is not confined to the area of worthwhile activities. It will be remembered, from my first lecture, that this is but one aspect of the moral life. There is also the area of role performances, social practices and the following of general social rules; there is the more interpersonal sphere in which emotions and motives have more place; finally, there is the sphere of 'will' in which virtues such as integrity, courage and determination are located. In these different spheres different levels of life can be distinguished which correspond roughly to the stages of moral development postulated by Piaget and Kohlberg which I also dealt with in my first lecture. But, having argued in the first part of this lecture both that the use of reason is a passionate business and that passions can be more or less reasonable, what I now hope to show is that these different levels of life involve not simply different capacities for reasoning but different types and levels of passion as well. By saying something about these different levels I hope to reinforce my thesis that the proper contrast is not between reason and passion but between different levels of life, each with distinctive levels of awareness and feeling.

(*a*) *Irrationality*

There is a level of life at which young infants live all the time and primitive people part of the time, which might be called a-rational in that it has not reached the level at which experience is structured by categories of thought associated with reason. More often, however, we describe it as irrational because we assume a lapse from a rational level on the part of a person who is capable of functioning at such a level.

This is the level of life with which Freud rather than Piaget was concerned. Piaget has attempted to sketch the various stages through which children pass on their ways to a rational form of life. Freud, on the other hand, was much more interested in the form of thinking which young infants exhibit, and which persists in adult life to interfere with and distort their more rational judgments and performances. He characterized it negatively in terms of the absence of categories of rational thought—for example, not observing the principles of non-contradiction, causality, and those defining a sense of reality. In my second lecture reference was made to Laing's account of the way in which schizophrenics lack a sense of their own identity and that of others, of the reliability of natural processes and the permanency of things (see p. 39). Positively Freud claimed that such thought followed the lines of the subject's wishes. As, however, he was much more interested in the vicissitudes of wishes deriving from the sex-instinct he did not elaborate the cognitive aspect of wishing. Later theorists such as Arieti, however, have done this. Arieti has noted the connection between such experience and a more primitive, palaeologic form of thinking in which classification is purely on the basis of the similarity of predicates without any importance being attached to the identity of the subject.[1] Wishing, in other words, goes along with a primitive, pre-Aristotelian form of thinking both in the minds of infants and some primitive peoples. This is frequent, too, in pathological states. The man, for instance, who flares up or behaves in an inappropriate way when confronted by an authority figure, is picking on one feature of similarity between his father, towards whom he had an aversion, and a whole succession of other men. Classification is based on affectively loaded similarity without regard to identity. In delusions, too, such as that of the girl who thinks that she is the Virgin Mary, the wish to be perfect can be connected with one point of similarity, virginity.

In considering cases like these one cannot say that the motivational element, as it were, determines the

[1] S. Arieti, *The Intrapsychic Self* (New York: Basic Books, 1967), pp. 109–12.

form of thinking; for even at this level the wish or aversion is connected with some features of a situation. But the feature is very faultily discriminated. There is not a wish or aversion for an object in the full sense of one that is identified by the normal subject-predicate form of thought. The inferences fasten on affectively laden similarities but take no account of differences. The cognitive and motivational aspects are bound together. The contrast is not between reason and a non-cognitive force that disrupts it. It is rather between a level of experience in which determinately conceived objects are wanted and realistic means taken to obtain them, and low-grade forms of experience, in which behaviour is influenced by wishes and aversions linked with primitive classification and thinking structured by some unconstrained thrust towards affinity of feeling.

At this level, too, emotions are based on a wild intuitive appraisal of the situation and, if the appraisals issue in behaviour, this does not attain the level of action in a full sense. Rather, it takes the form of emotional reactions, as when someone sitting in a chair looks up and takes what he sees to be a face at the window and gives an involuntary jump or cry. In such emotional reactions there is, on the one hand, a wild and fragmentary perception of the situation as in the cases of palaeologic thinking already mentioned; on the other hand, the movements made tend to be of a crude, protopathic type, lacking the co-ordination involved in deliberate action. Such emotional flare-ups often distort actions and performances, as when a teacher imagines some threat or criticism in the tone of voice of a pupil and reacts quickly with some person-centred jibe which does nothing to further the understanding of the point under discussion. In the case of the paranoiac this attitude of mind is a permanent one. The behaviour of others is persistently mis-read along this threat-laden, self-referential dimension. Here again it is not a case of a reasoning process simply being disrupted by an emotional reaction deriving from insecurity. Rather, it is a case of a level of life, in which the perception of the situation is structured in terms of determinate purposes and what I have called 'the rational passions', which help to keep the performer's eye on the ball, being replaced by another level of reactions which has its own cognitive and affective components.

At this level of life, too, there is a singular absence of 'will' and of those virtues such as determination and integrity which are connected with it. Indeed, it is the influence of such a level of life on behaviour that is one of the main explanations of lack of 'will'. The psychopath is, as it were, intellectually aware of the future and of the probability of punishment, which he does not want, if he satisfies a wish immediately and in some anti-social way. But he must have it now. He cannot delay the satisfaction of his wish. And what he lacks is not just social or moral concerns which might exert a countervailing influence. He lacks also some of the rational passions which go with the operation of reason—the conviction that he must take account of the facts, that the present, in itself, is not of overwhelming importance in relation to the satisfaction of desire. He lacks, in other words, the passionate side of Sidgwick's axiom of prudence.

(b) *Unreasonableness*

Piaget distinguishes two stages through which people have to pass on their way to the stage of autonomy at which they can reason about rules and adapt their behaviour in the light of views about their importance and validity. The first is the egocentric stage at which rules are seen purely as things that have to be done in order to avoid punishment or to obtain rewards. The second is the transcendental stage at which rules are conceived of as being 'out there', as part of the order of the world, but as supported purely by the sanctions of peer-group and parents. At both stages conformity to rules tends to be what Passmore calls 'toil'. There is no joy in it; the motivation is purely extrinsic—either expediency or desire for approval and fear of disapproval.

At both these stages there is a tendency for individuals to be unreasonable although they are capable of certain forms of reasoning. Indeed, unreasonableness is only possible for people who are capable of reasoning to a certain extent. It is exhibited by those who act in the light of reasons of a very limited type, whereas irrationality is exhibited by those whose beliefs or actions fly in the face of reason. The unreasonable man is a person who, in a situation in which there are a variety of relevant considerations, sticks fast to some consideration without giving due weight to others. He has reasons for what he thinks or does, but they are rather weak. There is the suggestion, too, that he does not pay much attention to the reasons or claims of others. He has a myopic viewpoint on the situation and takes little account of wider considerations. Or, on the other hand, he might simply be a conformist who sticks rigidly to what others say or do without ever pondering further about its rationale. Notions such as 'biased', 'bigoted', 'arbitrary' and 'obtuse' have application at this level of life.

The connection of being unreasonable with ego-centricity is obvious enough. There is lacking even the stability in behaviour which comes from acting in the light of established beliefs and practices. Beliefs tend to be infected with arbitrariness and particularity. Little attempt is made to fit them into a coherent system. And behaviour is governed largely by wants and aversions of an immediate, short-term character. Little account is taken of the viewpoint or claims of others. Indeed, the behaviour of others is seen largely in a self-referential way as it impinges on, threatens or thwarts the demands of the greedy, restless ego. The emotional life is not organized by means of stable sentiments. Rather, it tends to be gusty, dominated by emotions such as anger, fear, jealousy, envy and lust. Vanity there is, perhaps, which shows itself in sensitivity to slights, but no sober pride in solid accomplishments. There is, too, a bastardization of the exercise of will, which issues in 'wilfulness', and 'obstinacy'. This bears witness to the relentless assertion of the self rather than to the influence of principles or long-term aspirations. This level of life is marked not just by a limited capacity for reasoning which is infected by myopia and bias; it also is unaffected by the rational passions such as impartiality, respect for persons and the love of consistency.

At the next stage, the 'transcendental' stage of 'moral realism', the love of order, of doing the right thing, is very much to the fore. The individual is far less egocentric and instrumental in his approach. His capacity for reasoning is enlarged because of the love of classification and the desire to fit things in, to order them within an established framework. But he is capable of being unreasonable in another dimension because of the sanctity attached to what is established, which is reinforced by his fear of disapproval. He can be dogmatic, prejudiced and censorious because what is right is, for him, what is laid down by the group or by someone in authority. He is capable of a range of emotions beyond the ken of the egocentric man—loyalty, trust and shame. He can show courage, determination and other qualities of will in sticking to the code which he so reveres. But he does so largely because of the shame or guilt which he would feel if he succumbed to temptation, because of his fear of disapproval. But there is something second-hand about his conduct and emotional life, a lack of authenticity. For he has not really made his roles, rules and reactions his own. His life is a kind of toil; he does what he must because of his need for approval; not because of his insight into its rationale. Or perhaps he enjoys doing it like playing a game; he delights in mastery and skill without bothering his head about whether it has any point.

(c) *Reasonableness and autonomy*

The third stage of morality is called by Piaget, following Kant, the autonomous stage. He characterizes it mainly by reference to the individual's ability to reflect and criticize rules. He can turn round on an established code and conceive of its being otherwise; he sees that the validity of rules depends upon reasons which are made relevant by principles such as impartiality and respect for persons. This does not mean, of course, that he must always reflect before he acts and ponder on the validity of a rule which he is applying; for such a man would be a moral imbecile without settled principles. It only means that he has thought about rules in this way and has a disposition to do so if he finds himself in a situation where changed circumstances intimate some adaptation of his code.

If this capacity for reflection is to be effective in a man's life another type of condition must be satisfied. He must be sensitive to considerations such as the suffering of others or fairness which are to serve as principles for him. For it is not sufficient to be aware that actions have certain types of consequences; he must *care* about the consequences. And if his form of life is to be truly autonomous his concern for such considerations must not be second-hand. As Hume put it: 'no action can be virtuous or morally good unless there is in human nature some motive to produce it distinct from the sense of its morality.' In other words there must be some feature of a course of conduct, which the individual regards as important, which constitutes a non-artificial reason for pursuing it as distinct from extrinsic reasons provided by praise and blame, reward and punishment, which are artificially created by the demands of others. It is the linking of rules of conduct with considerations like these, which give point to it, that distinguish it from what Passmore calls 'toil'.

At this level of life emotions also become transformed by the capacity for reflection and criticism of the sort sketched earlier. Self-examination is possible not just in order to eradicate false beliefs but also in order to examine to what extent emotions such as envy, resentment and pride are compatible with fairness, respect for persons and concern for others. There is also the demand for authenticity associated with autonomy—the attempt to ascertain what one really feels as distinct from what one is expected to feel. The attack on *mauvaise-foi* is just one aspect of this general demand for authenticity. It is surely unintelligible without the Socratic conception of 'the care of the soul' —the inward application of the conviction that truth matters. The outward manifestations of this are to be found in a certain type of strength of will, in the form of courage and integrity which is characteristic of this level of conduct. For the individual has to hold fast very often against those same inclinations which at the previous level inclined him towards conformity to a code. He may have to resist disapproval, social ostracism, bribes, punishment and ridicule. He can only stand his ground if he has genuine and strong feelings about considerations which function as principles in his life. He must, for instance, have a genuine concern for truth, for fairness, and for the claims and point of view of others.

CONCLUSION

Enough, I think, has been said to sustain and illustrate the main thesis of this lecture—that the use of reason is a passionate business and that the emotional life can be more or less reasonable. Instead, too, of the usual contrast between reason and passion I have substituted that between different levels of life each characterized by distinctive levels of awareness and feeling.

I do not wish, of course, to hold up reasonableness as the *summum bonum* or anything as pretentious as that. Not only does that sound a bit quaint; for to call a man reasonable is not to praise him very highly. It also goes against the whole tenor of my first lecture in which I stressed the complexity of the moral life. Reasonableness, rather, is to be understood as a way of going about life which is compatible with all sorts of different emphases, with the pursuit of a variety of excellences. A man's abiding passion may be for music, science or for the political life. Reasonableness would not require that he should damp it down; only that he should not be completely oblivious to the claims of others, and that his personal relationships should not be shot through with contempt, envy, or paranoiac preoccupations. Alternatively his absorbing interest may be in his family and personal relationships. And why not provided that he is not derisive about those who become explorers or pilots? Reasonableness surely requires only a manner of travelling, not any particular destination.

Neither am I suggesting that anyone can live at this level of life all the time. It is a matter always of more or less. Even the most reasonable people are, at times, at the mercy of the infant that lives on in all of us, as Freud has shown. They have bouts or flashes of arbitrariness and egocentricity as well. And much of their conduct is still regulated by a customary code. They have not perhaps pondered long and deeply on the rights and wrongs of incest. They cheerfully stand in queues without weighing up the considerations which make this practice fair. Even Socrates seems to have had somewhat traditional thoughts about his wife. Manifestly, however, few people attain this level of conduct even in our own society. And those who do, seem to manage it without the degree of reflection and discipline required to become a Platonic guardian or to enter into Spinoza's state of human blessedness. For others, however, such as Spinoza, Kant and Whitehead, the life of reason is intimately connected with a religious view of life. This raises the question of the relationship between a rational form of morality and religion, which will be the subject of my final lecture.

Lecture Four

THE RELIGIOUS DIMENSION
OF A RATIONAL MORALITY

INTRODUCTION

MY account of a form of life, which has been called the life of reason, has so far been very limited. Little has been said about the details of its content—whether or not the individual is likely to be a doctor or a docker, whether he devotes his spare time to gardening or to golf, and what stand he takes on pornography, the pill, or the increase in world population. This might seem a defect to the practically minded; but it is a defect inherent in philosophy itself. The task of the philosopher is not to lay down in detail a code of conduct, but to attempt to arrive at considerations which are relevant in determining what such a code should be. Even as philosophy, however, my treatment has been limited, for although such considerations have been made explicit, no attempt has been made to justify them. The principles supporting the life of reason have been claimed to be general presuppositions of justification, so that anyone who believes that the unexamined life is not worth living is, *ipso facto*, committed to them. The details of this form of life have been developed to show that there is a middle way between being confined to a code and deciding things for oneself, between relying on authority and doing one's own thing, and between the life of toil, in which gratification is delayed, and the cult of instancy. They are implicit in a rational morality based on principles, in autonomy, and in the pursuit of worthwhile activities.

It might be said, however, that this form of life must be hostile to religion; for, in the end, religions are based either on authority or on revelation, and both these grounds of conduct are anathema to anyone who is committed to reason. So either a rational man will reject claims emanating from this source or he will maintain that, in certain spheres of life, he relies on faith. I have neither the time, nor the inclination to discuss this general issue at length. All I propose to do is to outline a personal position in the hope of showing that those are not the only alternatives for a reasonable man.

I THE FORM OF RELIGIOUS EXPERIENCE

The basic difficulty, presented by religion to any reasonable person, concerns objectivity, which is crucial to the use of reason. In science there is a particularly strong form of objectivity. Scientific terms are defined fairly carefully so that assumptions can be stated clearly and in ways which enable individuals from a variety of cultural backgrounds to reach a common understanding. And this is largely because the terms can be anchored firmly down to shared human experiences made possible mainly through the senses of sight and touch. Statements are thus made which can be tested by any normal observer. These are 'objective' in the strong sense that they are experiences of visible and tangible objects which exist independently of any particular observer, and which provide a basis for agreement in judgments.

Objectivity in rational morality is not quite as strong as this. It depends on a much looser agreement about the meaning of terms, on the acceptance of principles such as truth-telling and impartiality, which are presuppositions of practical reason, and on certain general features of human nature deriving from man's sociality and his aversion to pain and frustration. A claim can be made for moral facts in the sense that, in making moral judgments, anyone who is a rational moral agent will take for granted the wrongness, for instance, of the intentional infliction of pain on another human being. But this is not quite so palpable as one line being longer than another, which is an example of a fact in science; for moral facts are not relations between objects in a world independent of men that can be seen by any normal observer under normal conditions. More of human reactions is built into them from the start, although they are common reactions deriving from a shared human nature. This was the point made by Kant in a more extreme way when he claimed that in science, although men impose categories such as causality on the world to make it intelligible, the truth of particular causal laws depends on features of the world which are independent of man; in the moral case, however, agreement in judgments depends upon man's rationality alone, not at all on features of the world which are independent of him. But there is objectivity in both cases because what is true or correct depends upon considerations which are independent of the idiosyncrasies of any particular person or group of persons.

Is there anything comparable to this situation in the religious sphere which provides conditions for objectivity? In virtue of what kinds of shared experiences do human beings come to agree about religious judgments? If it is said that this is in virtue of religious facts such as the sacredness of human personality or the divinity of love, how are we to take notions such as 'sacred' and 'divine'? There are, of course, many different answers to this key question. Mine must necessarily be brief and unsupported by considerations taken from the philosophy of religion about the meaning and truth of religious statements, which it presupposes. It is, in fact, one which most religious people would regard as gravely deficient in what it leaves out, although acceptable, perhaps, as a beginning for what it puts in.

Religion, as I understand it, originates in experiences of awe, an emotion to which human beings are subject when they are confronted with events, objects, or people which are of overwhelming significance to them but which seem, in some important respect or other, inexplicable or shot through with contingency. Thus the cult of Jahveh, from which the Hebrew religion sprang, was connected in its early days with the awe evoked by volcanoes in their consciousness; for in the beginning the God of the Jews was a fire-god. Hence the significance of fire in the story of Elijah's confrontation with the priests of Baal. It can readily be imagined how living in the presence of such terrifying phenomena led the Hebrews to think of God in terms of stark contingency. 'I am what I am'.

The appropriate response to such a situation, which goes with the feeling of awe, is that of worship. Central to worship is the attempt to express the sense of the impressiveness and significance of the object of awe. Worship endorses such feelings, especially if it takes the form of public rituals, in the same sort of way as public mourning endorses the feeling of grief at the death of a relative. Indeed, there is a sense in which nothing appropriate can be done by someone who experiences awe and grief which parallels running away in the case of fear or aggressive behaviour in the case of anger. For the situation is not one which can be altered or remedied by appropriate action. All that the individual can do, therefore, is to express how he feels in some symbolic form such as prostrating himself, praying, or singing.

In undeveloped religions the objects of awe, which are infected with contingency, tend to be the powers of nature, exceptional people, impressive events, and so on. Worship proper is often interspersed with primitive types of petition and magic, which are attempts to placate mysterious beings, who are imagined as being responsible for the phenomena, or to alter the course of events by public expressions of human wishes. With the development of science and other forms of rationality, however, such phenomena and events become explicable and awe no longer attaches to them in their disconnected form. They become part of the orderly system of events that we call the universe.

But this type of development in human consciousness makes possible a more general type of object or situation for such feelings. For it comes to be appreciated, as it was pre-eminently by Kant, that in thinking about the universe we reach the limits of human reason. If we ask questions about its creation, or about its continuance, or about why there should be this type of system rather than some other, we grasp that we are posing questions which admit no answer in terms of the type of equipment that we have for answering questions. For although we can think about abstract possibilities in terms of purely logical principles, when we think about existing events and their explanation we are constrained to think in terms of a spatio-temporal framework within which certain types of generalizations are true—that is, causal generalizations. Yet we are demanding explanations of the type of framework which is a presupposition of all our explanations. And to grasp this is to open up the possibility of a new level of awe which is possible only for a rational being who appreciates the limits of reason. As Whitehead put it:[1]

God is the ultimate limitation and his existence is the

[1] A. N. Whitehead, *Science and the Modern World* (Harmondsworth: Penguin Books, 1938), p. 208.

ultimate irrationality. For no reason can be given for just that limitation which it stands in His nature to impose. God is not concrete, but He is the ground for concrete actuality. No reason can be given for the nature of God, because that nature is the ground of rationality.

To use the word 'God' in connection with the appreciation of this ultimate contingency of the world is to suggest that it is this general situation which calls forth awe. Not all reflective people who range round in this way at the limits of human understanding, are prepared to use the word 'God' to mark the experiences which they have, often because of the association of the word with a theism which they have outgrown. But in what ways does their religious response *differ* from that of the theist?[1] What extra work does the postulation of a spirit behind the phenomena do? Is it really necessary to express the awe one feels about the contingency, creation and continuance of the world in these personal terms?

Are there, however, any other experiences which call forth this feeling of awe in a rational man? Some are so impressed by the contingency of particular events that happen to them, that are of overwhelming importance, that they see the hand of God in them. Some feel this so strongly that they speak of being 'called', of being shown a sign, and so on. But these types of conviction are somewhat idiosyncratic, especially amongst more reflective people. More universal is the feeling of awe

---

[1] See J. Wisdom, 'Gods', in A. G. M. Flew (ed.), *Logic and Language*, 1st series (Oxford: Blackwell, 1952).

which Kant experienced when he thought about the position of man in a world which exhibited the order described by Newton's laws. For man, though part of the kingdom of nature, is able to understand why events take place as they do and to regulate his behaviour in the light of this understanding. In the moral sphere, too, man conforms to an order mainly of his own making. And because of these exercises of his reason, man is a free agent, a member of a kingdom of ends, as well as of a kingdom of nature. These thoughts about man occasioned in Kant respect for men as persons and awe at man's unique position in the natural world. And, in my view, the later discoveries of Darwin have done little to diminish the intensity of this feeling or to undermine its appropriateness: 'When I consider thy heavens, the work of thy fingers, the sun and moon which thou hast ordained, what is man that thou art mindful of him, and the son of man that thou considereth him?'

What is called Christian love can be understood as an intensified and particularized form of this generalized respect for the individual and awe that is felt for the predicament of any man trying to make something of his life. We are born. We grow up and gradually our predicament dawns on us. We have to make something of the brief span of years that is our lot, with the variable and partly alterable equipment with which we are blessed. To view another trying to make something of himself in this context, and to be intensely concerned about him is to love him in the Christian sense. And, of course, it is a very difficult attitude to sustain or to extend to many whom we meet. For our attitudes towards others are usually much more mundane and self-referential. For the Christian, however, this concern for other individuals is not only selfless. It is also a shared experience which unites a worshipping community. 'I live, yet not I but Christ liveth in me'.

For me, therefore, religious experience does not suggest a special kind of experience, akin to telepathy or clairvoyance; rather, it suggests a different level of experience made possible by concepts which enable us to understand the facts of a more mundane level of experience in a new light. It is a common-place in philosophy that all seeing is seeing *as*. What we experience, be it a cat or a calamity, is seen as such in part because of the concepts and expectations which we bring to it. Similarly, there is no action that is simply a bringing about of a change in the world; for what a man is doing depends upon the aspect under which he views particular movements and changes. In raising his hand is he signalling to a friend, testing the direction of the wind, or performing some ritual? It follows, therefore, that an experience, such as meeting another person, can be interpreted and enjoyed at very different levels depending upon what the individual brings to it. Activities, such as gardening, can be viewed as just keeping the place tidy, making it more beautiful, or even as a form of worship.

What, then, would convert an activity like gardening, which might be thought of in a very mundane way, into a religious activity? It would be the tendency to view it in a certain light, to connect it with some very general view of the natural world, which would vest this activity with a very different type of significance. And this would affect the manner of acting. People who garden for the glory of God go about it in a very different way from those who do it just for profit. This is tantamount to saying that a religious person is one who has developed a deeper dimension in his consciousness, which transforms his more mundane experiences. For a rational person this dimension is provided by the background awareness of the situation of man in the world which has awakened his awe. Thus particular chains of cause and effect, which he discerns in the natural world, will be haunted by the awe which he feels for the contingency of the natural order. Heracleitus's saying that character is destiny will not be just a psychological generalization but an awesome fact about man's position in the world. And human history will appear as a meeting place of man's will and foresight and of causal sequences that he has neither foreseen nor intended. Compassion will appear not just as a joyous, transforming type of experience, but as an all-pervasive bond between individuals that helps them to share their predicament in the world—the inescapable cycle of the human condition, birth, youth, reproduction, bringing up children and death, together with its contrasts such as joy and suffering, hope and despair, good and evil. As Whitehead put it:[1]

[1] A. N. Whitehead, *Religion in the Making* (Cambridge University Press, 1926), p. 60.

In its solitariness the spirit asks, what in the way of value, is the attainment of life. And it can find no such value till it has merged its individual claim with that of the objective universe. Religion is world-loyalty.

This concentration of consciousness in the face of the world may take the form of worship if the individual is moved by awe at certain aspects of it. He may feel the necessity to join with others, to express with others how he feels. He may also join with others in this way as a matter of determined policy. For he knows only too well the massive momentum of the mundane. The preoccupations of daily living crowd in. It is only too easy for the religious dimension of life to fade into the background, to emerge only fleetingly when some dire event activates it. The individual can become obsessed with obtaining some new possession, upset by some petty slight, or preoccupied with overtaking other people on a motorway. He may fail to ask himself, caught up in the fever of the moment, what, in the way of value, this adds to the attainment of life. There are few who can sustain this cleansing of the inward realms of consciousness without regular discipline.

2 THE RELIGIOUS DIMENSION OF MORALITY

Having sketched, somewhat falteringly, what I take religious experience to be, I must now briefly examine its relationship to the different aspects of the moral life set out in the preceding three lectures.

(a) Rational morality

The Stoics used to say that a man should alter what is

bad and alterable in the human condition and learn to live with and accept what cannot be altered. There are limits to the assertion of will and to the fixing of things for human benefit. Behind this thoroughly reasonable attitude to life lie two ultimate values which underpin the system of rational morality which I have put forward. On the one hand is the value derivative from man's sociality, his compassion and the demand that the human condition should be ameliorated in so far as it is possible. On the other hand is the allegiance to truth, the determination to see things as they are, to grasp the givenness of life. The fundamental principles of fairness and truth-telling, freedom and respect for persons are articulations of these ultimate values. Religious experience, so it seems to me, does not supersede these values, but by widening the context in which human life is viewed, has the function of enhancing our conviction of their objectivity and of providing emphasis for some of these values.

The function of religious experience in strengthening the objective status of moral values can be seen in its concentration on certain features of life and in its investing of them with universal significance. A cardinal feature of life, for instance, is pain, suffering and death. What is an appropriate response to this predicament? All the major religions write some response to this into their doctrine. One superficial view is that it is brought on the individual or the community by wrong-doing. The Book of Job is a magnificent protest both against this convenient assumption and the even more starry-eyed one that all is for the best in the best of all possible worlds. And when God says to Job 'Where was't thou, when I laid the foundations of the earth?' God's power is dramatized, as well as human ignorance and the fact that foundations support both the rainbow and the locusts.

To others evil seems essential to the nature of the world, or simply a partial perspective on life which is due to man's limited capacities for understanding. In Buddhism escape can only be found in release from individuality which is the vehicle of fragmentary and partial experience. Spinoza saw blessedness in attaining nearer and nearer to God's view of nature which is to see it as a pattern of interconnected events in which the reason for everything is understood. Such religious systems of thought stress the givenness of the world and the importance of understanding how things are. Truth matters supremely, but there is a fatalism about pain and suffering.

Thus religion, by placing the fact of suffering in a cosmic context, objectifies the particular response to it that is thought appropriate. It elevates some response to the badness of suffering, or to the importance of truth, which feature in any developed ethical system, to a more substantive status. Human beings are thought of as co-operating with, or surrendering themselves to some tendency in the nature of things. Attitudes appropriate to worship are called forth by the setting in which the response to suffering or to truth is placed.

Christianity has its own distinctive response to pain

and suffering. By its personification of love it suggests a way which is open to all to face the human predicament with some kind of hope. For the natural expression of love is to share as well as to try to remedy what seems irremediable, to shed our Stoic shells of self-sufficiency in the vivid realization that we are all members one of another. The kingdom of heaven is amongst us, not just within us. And often such sharing is as near to a remedy that we will ever get. The life and death of Jesus vest this response with some kind of ultimate significance. Indeed, as was stressed in the first lecture, this way of interpreting concern for others may be at the expense of other moral principles such as justice.

Indignation at the plight of the poor and oppressed is a comparatively recent response in the history of man, which has coincided with the realization that many ills are alterable by human effort. The Stoics accepted too much because they had too limited a view of what can be altered. The Christian response to suffering, too, was too personalized and piecemeal because it was not appreciated that much of it is a by-product of economic practices and social institutions that are alterable. The belief in progress began to get a grip on the minds of men—especially in the nineteenth century with the rapid growth of technology. Straight-forward theism faded, but in its place doctrines about a spirit or principle working through human history supported the belief in perfectibility, in the eventual abolition of suffering by human effort and ingenuity. Nature and economic forces were thought of as the enemy by Marxists. Human nature would come into its own in the kingdom of history when the kingdom of nature had been controlled. Thus the Marxist feels that he is part of a historic process; he experiences something akin to awe as he accepts necessity and finds freedom in subservience. The romantic, on the other hand, thinks of nature as the source of all that is good. It is human institutions that corrupt. Perfection is to be found in allowing what is natural to emerge.

Thus both progressives and romantics often endorse their belief in man and in the inevitability of progress and invest it with religious significance, even though they attack the religions that keep men in chains. Man's strivings are placed in the context of history or of the natural order of which he is claimed to be part. But Pelagian aspirations, be they individual or social, have usually been counteracted by Augustinian warnings against too much pride in human powers, too much trust in human knowledge, and too much assertion of the human will. The Greeks felt this strongly and Aeschylus expressed it magnificently in his variations on the theme of human ὕβρις. The doctrine of original sin is only superficially to be understood as a diatribe against human lusts and selfishness. It is to be seen more as a standing warning against the individual and collective pride of the human race. There is, after all, the givenness of the human condition and of certain facts of human nature. In the light of this any form of human perfectibilism is a dangerous delusion. There have been a few saints and heroes but, in the main, men are not like that. To dream of utopias on earth is vain; for they are not possible. And it is dangerous; for men will do dreadful things to other men in order to make their dreams come true.

Man's ὕβρις can even take the form, as it did in pragmatism, of the suggestion that truth is what furthers human purposes. But man is not the measure of all things. Even Bertrand Russell was moved to accuse the pragmatists of a cosmic impiety. He was sensitive to the givenness of the world and to the necessity for humility in the face of it. Much of the modern protest against the destruction of the environment derives from similar roots. Who is man to slaughter the elephants and the blue whale in his endless search for profit and human comfort? Who is he to fell the trees and foul up the mountains with his jerry-built chalets and his sprawling cable-cars? Utilitarianism, of course, has a place in human life. The elimination of misery is incumbent on anyone who cares about the human condition; the promotion of happiness is, in moderation, a harmless hope. But if this is the touchstone by which all else is to be judged, then this is impious as well as idiotic.

Religion thus has the function of endorsing and of emphasizing one or other of the fundamental principles of morality by placing its operation in a setting which awakens awe. It can also emphasize the importance of one or other of the areas of the moral life which were distinguished in the first lecture. Historically speaking some forms of Christianity have sanctified man's social position, his station and its duties, by the doctrine of stewardship. Society was seen in the Middle Ages almost as a mystical body, varying in order and degree, but dignified by participation in the common and hierarchical life of Christendom. Protestantism endorsed, in religious terms, the desirability of social mobility, of the individual making his own way by his own efforts. The priesthood of all believers, with its belief in autonomy, its tendency towards anarchism, and its ambivalence towards authority, also mirrored the growing demands for freedom and equality and the tensions inherent in the notion of government by consent. But, in spite of Hobbes likening the state to a mortal God, it has only been in modern times with the growth of nationalism that the state itself has been the object of the sort of awe that has usually been felt for God.

More often perhaps, Christianity has exalted the sphere of morality that is concerned with personal relationships; for the Christian emphasis on love is more at home in this sphere than in the more public, impersonal realm of civic duty. Indeed, there are many who argue that Jesus, because of his belief in his second coming, was singularly indifferent to the institutional aspects of morality. And certainly those, like St Francis, who seemed best to recapture the spirit of his life, felt the presence of God supremely in their personal dealings with others. It has been the church and Christian rulers, rather than Jesus himself, who have been acutely sensitive to the divine dimensions of institutional duties.

In contrast, however, to the emphasis on love there has been, ever since the time of Paul, an emphasis on the sphere of morality that is concerned with the will. The struggle for saintliness or salvation in the face of temptation has always been a central theme of Christianity. Indeed, the Kantian doctrine, that no one can be good by luck, that it requires a constant effort of will, comes straight down from Augustine. This emphasis reached its zenith in Puritanism. As, however, this is closely connected with autonomy, with the third stage of the development of morality with which I have been concerned in previous lectures, this deserves separate treatment.

(*b*) *Autonomy*

Religion, especially Puritanism, has done much to endorse and objectify the autonomy of the individual. No one has written more eloquently on this subject than Tawney in his *Religion and the Rise of Capitalism* in which the Puritan's lonely quest for salvation is emphasized.[1] He conveys vividly the way in which religious doctrines strengthened the sense of striving for perfection and individual self-sufficiency.

> When earthly props have been cast down, the soul stands erect in the presence of God. . . . The fire of the spirit burns brightly on the hearth; but through the windows of his soul the Puritan, unless a poet or a saint, looks on a landscape touched by no breath of spring. What he sees is a forbidding and frost-bound wilderness rolling in snow-clad leagues towards the grave — a

[1] See R. H. Tawney, *Religion and the Rise of Capitalism* (Harmondsworth: Penguin Books, 1938), especially pp. 227–30.

wilderness to be subdued with aching limbs beneath solitary stars. Through it he must take his way alone.

And Tawney, whilst bringing out so vividly the religious setting for this belief in autonomy, grasped equally vividly the irreligious perils of this particular version of it.

> Those who seek God in isolation from their fellowmen, unless trebly armed for the perils of the quest, are apt to find, not God, but a devil, whose countenance bears an embarrassing resemblance to their own. The moral self-sufficiency of the Puritan nerved his will, but it corroded his sense of social solidarity.

He was a spiritual aristocrat who sacrificed fraternity to liberty. In his search for perfection he shut off his spirit from the love of God and of his neighbour.

A similar sort of point can be made about some modern versions of the idealization of autonomy. In Sartre's doctrine, for instance, which is avowedly atheistic, the freedom of the individual to make himself by his choices is given some universal significance in the order of the world by the distinction between 'Being in itself' and 'Being for itself'. But the Other is seen by Sartre always as an enemy, whose look freezes us. We try to get others to recognize our freedom; but we also wish to manipulate them, to regard them as things, to possess ourselves of them. 'Hell is the other fellow'. The individual's quest for authenticity is as much a denial of the possibility of love as the Puritan search for salvation.

The autonomy of the individual, however, can be

endorsed in a way which is compatible both with a shared background of experience and with openness to love. The belief in the sacredness of human personality affirms in religious terms the principle of respect for persons, which is the appropriate attitude towards an individual who has the potentiality for determining his own destiny by his choices. Every individual has a point of view on the world, a perspective fixed by his unique stream of experience. He has his hopes and aspirations; he takes some pride in his achievements, however puny; and he has to choose, to make something of himself in the stark situation in which every man is placed. His person-hood matters supremely. It is not just a matter of not causing him unnecessary pain; for animals also should be regarded in this light. It is a matter of not manipulating him for our own purposes, not treating him purely as a functionary or occupant of a role, of not despising him as one who, like ourselves, mirrors the world from a particular point of view. Animals do not, in this sense, have a point of view. They are not aware of the past and future; they have no capacity for evaluation and choice; they are conscious but not self-conscious. To be aware of these facts about people and to care is to have respect for them as persons. And respect passes into reverence and a belief in the sacredness of human personality when the perspective and purposes of a particular man are viewed in the broader context of human life on earth.

But in speaking, as Kant did, of reverence for human

beings as persons, we are not just drawing attention to the unique point of view of every man. We are also indicating the potentiality for all to grasp a public predicament from their own stand-point and to do this through shared concepts and a shared form of understanding:[1]

> The great rational religions are the outcome of the emergence of a religious consciousness which is universal, as distinguished from tribal, or even social. Because it is universal, it introduces the note of solitariness. Religion is what the individual does with his solitariness.

In dealing with autonomy in the moral sphere in earlier lectures, the point was made that what is central to it is genuineness deriving from first-hand sensitivity to considerations such as fairness, and concern for people's suffering, that are picked out by principles. It is a rejection both of externally imposed standards and of second-hand judgment. But this does not necessarily imply that the considerations, in the light of which judgments are made, are not public ones that others can share with equal genuineness. In science we may insist on testing something for ourselves; but we do so with our eyes, and we fasten on features that others, too, can see with their eyes. The same applies in the religious sphere. We may become vividly aware of aspects of situations as individuals; but others, too, share the concepts which enable us to see situations in this light.

[1] A. N. Whithead, op. cit., p. 47.

So the autonomy of the individual need not take the form, as depicted by Tawney, of the lonely quest for salvation. No doubt many believers in individual autonomy are over-preoccupied with their own saintliness; but salvationism and the quest for individual perfection does not seem to me to be characteristic of a religious body that values autonomy such as the Society of Friends at its best. The concentration is rather 'out there', on evils such as slavery, war and poverty. And even in such practical matters, although there is sympathy and encouragement for individual concerns, the insistence is always that these shall be publicly entered into and discussed. The refusal to decide things by vote, the insistence on getting the sense of the meeting, institutionalize both the emphasis on corporate action and the conviction that individual insight must be tested by reference to shared criteria.

(c) *Worthwhile activities*

In this lecture I have not been much concerned with religion in general which would cover phenomena as disparate as Baal worship, Buddhism and perhaps Marxism. I have mainly concentrated on the type of religion which might be acceptable to a person capable of a rational level of life. In dealing, therefore, with worthwhile activities, I will confine myself to the difference that a religious dimension to a man's consciousness might make to life at this level. In the third lecture its main features were claimed to be the transforming of ordinary activities, such as those of friendship or travelling, by the understanding and sensitivity that are brought to them, the choice of activities that permit plenty of scope for this (for example, science or friendship rather than rubbing one's back on the bark of a tree), the concentration on the quality of life which is given by the standards immanent in activities which are required by their point, the rational attitude to time which rejects both the cult of the instant and that of the future or the past, and finally, the transforming of all activities by the concern for truth. How would an individual's reflections, in the situation of solitariness, to which Whitehead constantly refers, affect his view of how he should spend his time?

First, I think, it would make him more acutely aware that this is a momentous issue that must be squarely faced. It must not be allowed, as it were, to creep up on him as he grows older, or to hit him unprepared at a critical moment in his life. He must grasp the ultimate pointlessness of life, that it cannot, as a whole, be given meaning in the way in which meaning is given to events and actions *within* life; but he must also strive to discern point within it. For life, like works of art, can exhibit values that are self-contained, that define a quality of life. Second, he will not feel that, in facing this issue, he is 'choosing' his values, or, like Lucifer, imposing them on the world. Rather, he will feel drawn towards them and, in so far as he lets them work through him, he will feel a sense of humility and of awe. A rational person will necessarily value truth. But if he is also religious, he will feel that he is merely a vehicle for something in human life which is of inestimable importance. He will appreciate only too vividly that there are strong tendencies within himself and within human beings generally, that incline towards distortion and suppression. He will appreciate, too, that there is little connection between truth and human happiness. But, in insisting that things must be seen as they are, he will feel that he is doing what he must, that he is responding to what is required by man's situation in the world. For his propensity to reflect, to make sense of things, is pointless without the pressure from the ideal of truth which draws him towards it.

A religious man will feel the same about the relief of suffering. He will know that some forms of suffering can only be endured and shared, not remedied. He will view with horror the utilitarian dream that eventually everything can be fixed up for human benefit; for suffering, in some forms, is just part of the human condition. Nevertheless, he will feel that, whatever the ultimate prospect, he must do what he can about it. And again, in so doing, he will feel that his response is demanded by the human condition, that he is allying himself with countless others who have seen what he has seen and not turned their backs. And if he is also moved by love for individuals and not just by respect for them or concern for them as sufferers, he may have a similar view of love. He may feel that an openness to love is demanded of him and that, in letting it work through him, he is merely a vehicle of a universal tendency that works for harmony in a world in which conflict is inevitable.

How then will this attitude to what he values most affect how a man spends his time? He may be lucky enough to obtain a job which is directly concerned with the advancement of truth or with the relief of suffering. Indeed, he may feel so drawn to some sphere of activity that he may regard this as his vocation, as the only thing in life that is worth doing for him. Like Socrates he may prefer death to abandoning it. But this way is not open to all. More usually these values will transform how a person conceives and carries out a job which is not directly concerned with promoting these values. If he is in business he may be insistent that no specious advertising is used, that there is no exploitation. He may strive to humanize the institution in which he works, and to treat others as persons and not just as functionaries. He may think of his place of work as a jumping off ground for the development of personal relationships. The same sorts of points could be made about family life and lesiure-time pursuits which it would be otiose to elaborate. The underlying thought is that activities can be transformed and enriched by the manner in which they are conceived and that most activities are very openended. One of the distressing features of modern industrial society is that there are so many tasks which are routine, monotonous and self-contained, giving little scope for this type of transformation. The job of the housewife is infinitely more varied and richer in its scope for such transformation than that of the average industrial worker.

Religion affects the individual's choice of activities

and the manner in which he conducts them by enlarging the context in which these activities are placed, by pressing the question whether this is all that a man can do with the brief flicker of consciousness that is his life. Awareness of this context in which human beings live their lives is a matter of degree and its development is, to a certain extent, a matter of will. Or at least, like the demands made on us by love, truth and suffering, it can be repressed or admitted to full consciousness. There are many who have glimmerings of it who immerse themselves in practical tasks. A vast man-made environment is created by means of which man is, to a certain extent, insulated from some of the features of life which bring his predicament too vividly home to him. Even funerals are advertised as if they were more or less expensive trips abroad. Others, like silkworms or butterflies, make the most of the instant, when their powers are at their height and their faculties undimmed. But it is all in vain; for the human predicament asserts itself with the meaninglessness of middle-age. For to learn how to live is also to learn how to die. Those who see this steadily can live each day as if it were their last because they can keep in their consciousness the context in which human life has to be lived. They can thus concentrate on the 'quality of life which lies always beyond the mere fact of life'.[1] They are, perhaps, entering the kingdom of heaven, and have some dim understanding of what might be meant by eternity.

[1] A. N. Whitehead, op. cit., p. 80.

j